# TWO STORIES

D. BRENT WEATHERLY

# Prologue

My dream was to be an author, but early on I realized that a career in software development was my best path to paying the bills. But, as fate would have it, it turns out I've been doing some writing this past year and a half, in the form of blog posts chronicling my battle with cancer. With the encouragement of many, I'm publishing them here, in more or less their original form.

For the purpose of context, let me provide some background. My blog site was originally created in order to provide updates to family and friends on a major surgery I was undertaking away from home at the MD Anderson Cancer Center. I expected to be in Houston for at least four weeks; and rather than my wife and I sending texts, emails and repeating ourselves in phone conversations, we chose, like many others, to setup a site for people to follow. I don't recall why I chose a blog site for this purpose instead of a more specific, health-related tool, but as I think about it now, it's as if we knew I was going to have a lot more to say as time went on than just updates from a presumed incident-free surgery and recovery. Because that is not what happened. I think it was my wife, probably, who had a feeling that life was only beginning to get complicated, and I would need more than just her pair of ears as a conduit for all the words that were to flow from what we were about to go through. It seems I would have need for writing in my life after all.

I discovered that writing the posts allowed me to talk about things I am struggling with, be it my health or my faith. I'm a somewhat private person, and talking to people about my life makes me uncomfortable. Writing allows me to deliver my thoughts one-directionally. But as I wrote, I found that my words seem to resonate with others beyond those personally interested in my cancer journey, as many related to the common struggles of life and the doubt and fear and questions about God. Both wanting to extend encouragement while at the same time receiving it, I expanded the scope of the posts beyond simple (or not so simple) health updates. And now, because of further prompting, I have chosen to publish these posts as a whole for those who prefer the printed format with a bookmark to occasional electronic digests.

As someone who had once aspired to be a writer of fiction, it was strange to find that my chance to publish was to be through essays, as some have referred to them, through a brief period of my life journey. As you'll see from the progression of the posts, this time was also about finding my voice, so the format, tone, subject, and, though I wish I could pretend otherwise, the quality changes from the start to the stopping point, but, again, these are the posts in mostly their raw form.

Surprisingly (and somewhat disappointingly), I found that my children did not want to read my posts. If I felt it important to share some of these words with them, I typically had to read them aloud. I understand, though. In their eyes, they are already living with my cancer, so there is no reason to read about it. But to me, I want them to read because I hope that some of what I'm saying will be of use to them some day. My fatherly advice, so to speak. Not knowing the future, this book may still be that.

The book's title, *Two Stories*, came about for two reasons. First, because, as you'll glean from the posts, they were a method to provide updates about my family's battle with my cancer, but I'm also using it to talk about my faith journey as a follower of Christ. Two stories. But, also, the title of my blog comes from a sermon, "The Two Stories," by the theologian and author, Frederick Buechner.

Being open and vulnerable about my health and my faith is no easy thing, and there have been many times that I have wanted to quit writing due to feelings of embarrassment, insecurity, and fear of judgement. Sensing this, my dear friend and pastor Jared Bryant pointed me to Mr. Buechner's writing, and this sermon in particular, because Jared thought it would resonate with me and encourage me. It certainly did. If you want to know what I'm about or, at least, what I hope to be about and think the whole world should be about, then I encourage you to read that sermon (it is available on Buechner's website).

Within it, Buechner writes,

> *"...to tell the story of who we really are and of the battle between light and dark, between belief and unbelief, between sin and grace that is waged within us all costs plenty and may not gain us anything, we're afraid, but an uneasy silence and a fishy stare."*

So, within the faith journey, there are the two stories of my life and Christ's and how they intertwine; and, to be sincere, despite my fears, I must tell both. But Buechner encourages me as he says, "each of us has a tale to tell if we would only tell it."

Starting with the surgery in the Spring of 2016, I find the lives of myself and my family have progressed through four seasons, and I've grouped the posts into sections accordingly. To help with flow, I'll begin each season with a summary of that time. I've tried not to alter the posts themselves, but notes and edits will be italicized.

I will mention several people by name in these posts, so I'll provide the common ones here:

**My family:**

**Wife: Kim**

**Children: Joy, Caroline, Samantha, Owen**

**10**

**Pastors: Don Aldin, Jared Bryant**

*Special thanks to my friends Morgan Cogswell and Katy Van Wyk for their design and editing help.*

# Survivor Story for GeorgiaCancerInfo.org

## *June 16, 2017*

*[Since my original diagnosis was in 2013 and the posts begin in 2016, there is obviously a lot of the story untold. But, though it seems odd to start the story three years into the battle, it would be inappropriate to write about the previous three years as a memoir when the posts tell the story, so to speak, as it unfolds. To provide a bit of background, though, I'll share a portion of a "survivor story" that I wrote for GeorgiaCancer.org for their cancer survivorship month in June. The article provides a brief summary of how the reality of my condition unfolded. I'll then provide some words I spoke to the congregation of our church back in February of 2014, which sheds some light on how we perceived God was at work even then.*

*Note: the full article is available at* https://www.georgia-cancerinfo.org/survivor-stories/.*]*

On April 11, 2013, the birthday of my twin daughters, I visited my gastroenterologist for a colonoscopy. At the time, I was going through some difficulties with my job, and I was experiencing symptoms I thought were consistent with an ulcer. At the age of 43, with no history of colon cancer in the family (though not long after my cousin would also be diagnosed), the GI doc presumed my symptoms were related to some minor ailment. Well, after the procedure, the doctor informed me that I had a growth in the lower part of my colon. He showed me a picture of a dark gray, abnormally shaped ball attached to the lining of my bowel. I remember his saying that he didn't think it was a major problem. I'd have surgery and maybe some chemotherapy but that this would be just a "blip" in our lives. My children were aged 12, 10, 10, and 8 at the time, so, despite being stunned and dazed by the news, my wife and I didn't have the luxury of processing time. We had to carry on with the "normal" stuff of life of a family of six, which, after the visit, began that very afternoon with a birth-day party for the twins.

The unfolding of the reality of my condition has been slow but seemingly always worse than we previously thought. Before the surgery, a CT scan didn't reveal much. We saw only the mass in my colon and maybe an enlarged lymph node or two in that area. However, the pathology report from the 16 lymph nodes that were removed during surgery showed that 13 of them were positive for cancer. So, the diagnosis was Stage IIIc. We digested that news, but were comforted that it wasn't Stage IV, and we put our hope in the efficacy of chemotherapy. After recovery, I received 6 months of FOLFOX, at the end of which a CT scan showed "no evidence of disease." Perhaps this would be just a blip.

Unfortunately, 6 months later at the oncologists's office following a CT scan, we discovered a small mass *outside* of my colon. A subsequent PET scan revealed cancer activity in distant lymph nodes, so the reality is that I was Stage IV from the journey's beginning. Summarizing all that has happened would take pages, but I've spent time at MD Anderson, received different therapies, undergone radiation, had surgeries, but ultimately it seems that cancer has a firm foothold in my body, though at this point it is mostly microscopic.

Fast-forwarding to today, the tumor still exists, and we're still fighting, now with experimental medicine from a phase Ib trial under the direction of an oncologist from the Sarah Cannon Cancer Center. The good news is that, as of the time of writing, the treatments have so far been effective.

# Living Church Speech

## *February 16, 2014*

*[Note: I spoke during a "Living Church" segment of a worship service at our church, Resurrection Presbyterian Church, in Athens, GA. At this time, I hoped that I was cancer-free, having had the original tumor removed from my colon and undergone standard first-line chemotherapy, at the end of which CT scans showed no sign of disease. I was unaware of the extent of unseen disease.]*

When Jared asked me to talk during a living church segment, I must confess I've been hesitant, not only because I would be nervous but also because I wouldn't be cool like some of the other guys who've done this, like those with a laid-back approach. I hadn't really thought about this, really, until I was having lunch with Don and he said something about my being serious... I guess that's true, but it certainly wasn't always this way.

A little history here: Prior to living in Athens, I had never been a member of a church. When we moved here, Kim and I went looking for a church home, not because I was seeking it but more because Kim was, and I had made a commitment to her to be a regular attendee of a church. We both really liked Redeemer and went through the new membership process, but I definitely had a lot of reservations and was struggling with belief. It all pretty much came to a head when we met with Pastor Hal [of Redeemer] to discuss our joining, and when it came my turn to tell my story, Hal really challenged me by allowing me to call myself an atheist. Naturally, we didn't join at that point. Then after many weeks of praying and struggling, it finally occurred to me that I had to make a choice to believe. I was not going to think myself into being a Christian. It was at that point that we joined Redeemer, and I certainly took the vows we were going to make very **seriously**.

Long story short: Kim and I became very involved at Redeemer. It is amazing how the world presents itself as created and sustained by a God when you open your eyes to see it, and I ultimately became a part of leadership there. It was about this time that Resurrection was getting started. I think I always knew that I wanted to be here and would ultimately be here, but at that time Kim really wasn't ready, and I wanted to fulfill my commitment as a Deacon to Redeemer, so we stayed. After a year or so, we made the decision to join Resurrection, and my primary reason for doing so is that the people I thought about most, prayed about most and really wanted to serve were here. Plus, I had this fear that my kids were just caught up in the "big church", primarily seeing only the social aspect of it. Not that there's anything wrong with that, of course, but I ultimately want them to understand what it means to belong to a church. Having removed them from their larger groups of friends their ages, I have been waiting for the day when they ask me, "Why did you bring us here?", and hopefully we would have a good answer for that.

A couple of years ago I led our community group. And for me it was a great experience for many reasons, but I really liked the theme of our sermon series of that time: "the wilderness". Those in our community group will remember that I like to make diagrams, and one of them was based on the wilderness theme where a traveler was trying to get to a place of "rest" along the road where many voices can be heard, some are helpful and some are not. I remember at that time, during sermons and reading the Bible, all I could think about was other people, family and friends that needed grace and mercy. How we needed to be voices to point them to Christ.

However, it was at the turn of the year, 2013, that I got diagnosed with cancer, and I began to think about *myself*...a lot. In fact, I began to have an identity crisis. What I call "big C" versus "little c" (or Christ versus cancer) for control of my heart and my mind. I was resolved to stay strong and faithful, but unfortunately every time we got new news, things were a little worse than we thought, and this began to allow my unbelief to resurface for me to battle with again. It was at this time, I think, that Don gave a sermon on the concepts of believing and belonging, and how both are so critical to the life of a Christian. And the two depend on each other to prevent us from hopeless despair and isolation. Well, enter the community of believers.

We were overwhelmed with support from the get-go, and I was blown away with the kindness of people visiting me in the hospital. One particular salve for my soul was when I was telling one gentleman how the doctors say that there is typically no cure for stage IV cancer [*at that point we thought I was late stage III*], and he reminded me how with God there is always a chance to cure because believers are always praying. Doctors do what they do and believers do what we do. God can act in natural and supernatural ways.

During recovery and then treatment, it seemed that whenever my belief or faith was weak, I got a text message, a phone call, a meal, or face-to-face fellowship, and it was the faith and belief in the power of prayer of those reaching out that really helped me. There were days I just didn't want to pray, or doubted that prayer worked, and I really got sick of praying for myself...felt guilty about it. At that time, other friends and family also became ill or had other struggles, and I needed to pray for them. Knowing that there were others praying on my behalf (as is Jesus) who didn't doubt one bit in the power of prayer and the presence of God made me finally get a real picture of the body of Christ. When my belief was weakening, belonging strengthened me. My identity in Christ and my being a part of His body are intertwined.

Now, we know that the church isn't perfect, but what do we mean when we say we are "building community"? To me, we are revealing the body of Christ, which is super powerful...and serious. I remember when we first moved to Athens, I would tell people that we really loved the city because the town is small enough where people mattered. When you met someone, there was a chance you'd see that person again, so your meeting wasn't meaningless. I like to think that heaven is an infinite small town.

This year, Don and Jared have been preaching on the idea of exile and restoration. Well, obviously I'm seeking restoration of my body and would love resolution to the problems that my friends and family are facing. I wish I could say I was cured already, and I don't need prayer anymore, but I still do. And I really appreciate it. I wish I could say that my prayer list for others has gotten shorter, as if I've checked off those who are okay now. Unfortunately, there are more people sick, and dear friends and family are still suffering with the struggles of life; we have to acknowledge that we are in exile in a fallen world. However, as Don said in last week's sermon, "the church is an outpost in the midst of exile". And further, "hope shapes what we do." Through all of this, the restoration we seek is not necessarily the restoration that God is undertaking. The blessing is going through these struggles together.

I say we came to Resurrection in hopes that my kids

would come to understand what the church was all about and what it meant to belong. As is often the case with missionaries on a mission who return saying that they personally were most impacted, it seems that God wanted to show me (and Kim too) what church and belonging really look like. I understand better now. And to my kids, I can say that the church, the community of believers, and the body of Christ have been so critical in helping me get through this past year. More than ever I desire to put my arms around people I see who are suffering and tell them that they matter. I pray that you experience that one day.

I've already gone too long, but I'll leave with this last story. It was right before Christmas, and I had received a blood test that scared me. I was cruising along and then the blood test rocked me. I felt the familiar fear and unbelief hit me. It was at that time that the son of friends of ours from Redeemer was in the hospital, and Redeemer held a prayer meeting on the Friday that I heard the news. I chose to go, just to be around fellow believers and pray for someone in need. As it turns out, someone with whom I guess you could say I struggle to love wound up in my breakout group for prayer. There was something healing about praying with him. Also, the week before the prayer meeting, I donated an old family table to a family in need. As I left the church after prayer, I was stopped by a friend of the family who encouraged me that the table had been a great blessing. And as I was getting in my car, standing alone in the parking lot was the man who had given me the strong encouraging words when I was in the hospital. I wouldn't always do this, but I got out the car to just chat. Is all of this just coincidence? To some, probably. But to me it reminds me that God is at work. And we get to be a part of it.

# *Season 1*

## *Surgery and Recovery*

As the first posts describe, the plan in April of 2016 was to have an abdominal surgery to remove a tumor and whatever it might be touching from the lower plumbing of my body. Unfortunately, the doctor, upon discovering the extent of disease, aborted the surgery and simply sewed me up after cutting me open. My memory of coming out of anesthesia is hazy, but I recall lying on a thin mattress under several blankets in a large, low-ceilinged post-op room that was clearly in the basement of the MD Anderson hospital. My wife was on my right and a nurse was on my left. All I remember is my wife's sweet and reassuring face telling me that they didn't remove the tumor and my screaming for them to return me to the O.R. to accomplish the goal for which we had been hoping, planning, and praying for the previous two years.

Then, a darkness set in, and I feel badly for the poor nurse who had to endure my despair, though I know that this must be a common and difficult part of that job. I have the utmost respect for healthcare workers now, I assure you. But even then, I recall a tension. Yes, I was in anguish, but I remember talking to her and other nurses and doctors about the power of God that I more accurately describe as not letting me go. It kept a hope alive in me as I began to accept a fate that, medically speaking, likely meant a terminal prognosis, even if the doctors never used such language. In fact, my surgeon told me "I had already beaten the odds" and that they didn't speak of the difficult ques-

*tion of longevity with me because of a concept they call "conditional survival" where the longer a person survives, the longer a person is more likely to survive. But the hope I had wasn't just about my health condition, it was also about my heart condition. My soul condition. I needed to believe that while my body is mortal, my soul is eternal. With these thoughts swirling in my head, I recovered from surgery in Houston, returned home to Bishop, GA, and kept on surviving. What follows is the first part of that journey.*

# The History of Our Battle

## *March 31, 2016*

*[This is the first blog post. It is now two years since I delivered the "Living Church" segment. Suffice to say, the blood test to which I referred was an indication that my battle with cancer was just beginning. This post quickly summarizes the previous three years prior to surgery to remove a recurrent tumor.]*

As I sit here with my sweet wife Kim at the MD Anderson Cancer center in Houston, awaiting an appointment with a doctor of internal medicine, Kim commented that it might be helpful to document the history of our battle with cancer. So here goes:

April 11, 2013: after having some strange GI symptoms for several weeks, I went in for a colonoscopy. I was then 43, and we were expecting nothing. Unfortunately, they discovered a walnut sized tumor in my sigmoid colon.

A CT scan showed what appeared to be 1 enlarged lymph node but not much else, so our oncologist was thinking I was probably stage IIc or IIIa.

April 25, 2013: had colon resection to remove the tumor at St Mary's hospital in Athens. Pathology showed that 13 of the 18 lymph nodes that were removed during surgery were positive for cancer. I was diagnosed as having Stage IIIc adenocarcinoma.

Mid-May 2013, we had our first visit to MD Anderson to get a second opinion on treatment options and to establish a relationship there.

At the end of May 2013, I began 6 months of chemotherapy with the FOLFOX regimen. The powerful agent in this protocol is Oxaliplatin, good at killing cancer cells but can also cause permanent neuropathy (tingling numbness in feet and hands). I continue to have neuropathy to this day, although it did get better with time.

September 2013: CT scan showed that I had no sign of cancer!

October 25, 2013: last round of chemo. I was a free man!

April 25, 2014: a follow-up CT scan showed a new node, about 1.5 cm outside of my rectum. It is assumed that this is a blood borne metastasis.

May 2014: we returned to MD Anderson to confirm that the spot was cancerous and for treatment options. A PET scan showed positive lymph nodes outside of the pelvic area, one as distant as my collar bone (lymphadenopathy). The diagnosis is that I have chronic colorectal cancer and will be on some sort of treatment the rest of my life.

Mid-May 2014, began 2nd round of chemotherapy using the FOLFIRI+Avastin protocol, primary agent is Irinotican.

Aug 2014: returned to MD Anderson for follow-up. Tests show the tumor has shrunk and lymphadenopathy had resolved (no longer metabolically active). Oncologist Dr Garrett suggests switching to maintenance treatment (no Irinotican)

Aug 2014–April 2015: chemo every two weeks.

April/May: began having GI symptoms again.

June 2015: excruciating abdominal pain and bloating lead me to the ER in Athens. CT scan at hospital suggests that my colon is almost 100% blocked by the rectal tumor. This was then confirmed by colonoscopy.

June 14, 2015: had temporary ileostomy installed to bypass blocked colon.

July-Aug 2015: had 28 radiation treatments to attempt to shrink/kill the abdominal tumor that was blocking my colon prior to forthcoming surgery.

Oct 2015: returned to MD Anderson for surgery to remove tumor. Unfortunately, a PET scan showed the lymphadenopathy (cancer of the lymphatic system) had returned, so they had to scrap surgery. Also learned my oncologist had left MD Anderson.

Returned to Athens and began FOLFIRI+Avastin chemotherapy again.

December 2015: PET scan shows cancer again responding to treatment. Most of lymphadenopathy had resolved, 2 other nodes in the peri-aortic area had shrunk and were not significantly active. Unfortunately, the cancer in my pelvis is still active, even after radiation.

New Year's Eve 2015: began urinating blood. After a week of this, a trip to a urologist in Athens showed what appeared to be cancer involvement with my bladder. This was confirmed by pathology. The urologist stopped the bleeding.

Late January: returned to MD Anderson to meet with surgeon and new oncologist for options. The surgeon still believes that surgery is best option for me. Surgery date set for April 14.

Feb 2016: CT scan showed continued response to treatment. Abdominal tumors (it was determined that there are actually 2 close together) are mostly stable and the peri-aortic lymph nodes had shrunk a bit more.

March 28–April 1 (Now): I'm here to meet with internal medicine and urologist and to get a PET scan to make sure the lymphatic cancer cells are still inactive...

What has sustained us thorough this battle? What has enabled me to continue to find joy? Hope. And faith.

Jesus says in John 16:7 "Nevertheless, I tell you the truth: it is to your advantage that I go away, for if I do not go away, the Helper will not come to you. But if I go, he will come to you." This Helper is the spirit of Christ, and he has strengthened me and given me peace to persevere. My body aches to be healed by the hand of Christ, but His spirit is doing a work in me and those around me that is far better than I can imagine.

Jesus also says in Matthew 16:18 "And I tell you, you are Peter, and on this rock I will build my church, and the gates of hell shall not prevail against it." Christ's church is often called His body, and in some mysterious way it is. And through the church, be it members of my local church, Resurrection Presbyterian, or through friends from our school from other churches, my family and I have been loved deeply. I, in turn, have sought to love and serve others, albeit very imperfectly. It is by serving and being served, in the act of following Christ, that life has true meaning and purpose. Thus with every new day we can rejoice together in our many blessings, even as we share in each other's sufferings.

The future of my health, as in all things in this physical world, is uncertain. But our hope is in the certainty that Christ has defeated death and has promised us eternal life.

Please realize that I continually forget this. As I write, I remember and choose to believe.

# Drum Roll Please...

## *April 5, 2016*

Folks, the PET scan came back with good news. Well, good news in the fact that I'm clear for surgery. The treatment continues to be effective in suppressing tumor growth, so I'm "stable/improved" everywhere except the area that needs surgery. But even my abdominal disease appears stable. Now is the time to go for clearing out that area.

Thanks for your prayers; we lean on them. Kim and I will now fly home from the Keys on Saturday, then fly back to Houston on Sunday. We'll be gone the rest of April most likely. Please pray for the surgery, of course, but also for my kids and Kim's parents, who'll be staying with them in our absence.

Peace and Grace

Brent

*Jesus, lover of my soul,*

*Let me to Thy bosom fly,*

*While the nearer waters roll,*

*While the tempest still is high.*


*Hide me, O my Savior, hide,*

*'Til life's storm is past;*

*Safe into the haven guide;*

*Receive my soul at last.*


*Other refuge have I none,*

*I helpless, hang on Thee;*

*Leave, oh leave me not alone,*

*Support and comfort me.*


*All my trust on Thee is stayed,*

*All help from Thee I bring;*

*Cover my defenseless head,*

*With the shadow of Thy wing.*

# It's On

## *April 11, 2016*

Hey folks. Thanks for the comments and the other forms of encouragement the past week or so. Kim and I just got to Houston.

Tomorrow will be a big day of tests and pre-op consultations. Though we had a great time with family in the Keys last week, it was sad to say goodbye to the family. Please pray for our kids and Kim's parents, who will be taking care of them, with the help of our many dear friends.

It was so nice to be able to go to church this morning. It was just Joy and me, but it was truly food for my soul. To see friends, get some hugs, and to hear a fantastic message from Pastor Jared was the ideal way to send me on our way.

In particular, he reminded us "to not forget the signs" that God is with us, even when we feel alone, lost, or too often failures in trying to live by faith. He was quoting from *The Silver Chair*, by CS Lewis, where Aslan reminds Jill to remember the signs that would keep her from faltering on her journey.

I haven't read the book, but I certainly related. I feel like God is always reminding me He's with me in crazy "coincidences." My problem is that I either want to over analyze and interpret the signs in order to know God's will, or I simply forget about them in difficult times and fear that God is not there are all.

Now that I'm away from home, family, and friends for at least 3 weeks for this surgery, I really need to re-member the signs. Especially that big one we celebrat-ed 2 weeks ago. Ya know, that whole empty tomb thing we celebrate at Easter...

Much love and humble appreciation,

Brent

# Long Day

## *April 12, 2016*

Greetings friends and family. Kim and I had a long but good day at MD Anderson today.

It started at 7 am with an MRI – 45 minutes of what seemed like rock concert percussion, synthesizers, and guitar jams. After this was blood work, followed by a consultation with the anesthesia group. Aside from the discomfort of the MRI, the morning was unremarkable.

We had our first meal of the day in "Cafe Anderson," and then met up with a friend who used to live in Athens and attended Resurrection with us. His family lives outside of Houston, and he works at MDACC.

We then had a consultation with the surgical oncology group, which took a while. There was still some discussion of whether surgery is the best option, but the surgeon strongly believes that it is, so that matter is finally settled. It is crazy to think of what all has to be done on Thursday. I'll go more into this tomorrow, but suffice to say, in our view this surgery seems very rare, so much so that even our oncologist in Athens told me "there's no one around here who can do this surgery." But during our consultation, the doctor matter-of-factly stated that he had performed the same surgery last Thursday! These folks are the best in the business, so that's reassuring.

After the visit with the surgeon, it was down the hall for a consultation with radiation oncology. A radiation oncologist will be on standby in case our doctor determines that I should receive radiation on an area, like a bone, for which the surgeon is unable to get clear margins (no evidence of cancer). MD Anderson has a single operating room that is equipped with a special radiation machine for direct application to diseased tissue while the patient is opened up during surgery. Again, reassuringly, I was informed that MDACC is one of only five hospitals in the country with this capability. And they do this about 10 times a month. Amazing.

Finally, at 4:30, we had an ostomy marking consultation. The purpose of this meeting is to identify the best location on my belly for the surgeon to install another ostomy bag. It was nice that we knew the man with whom we met, as he marked me last June for the first ostomy. He was very encouraging that living with these bags is more common than one might think, and I can do most anything with them.

We were exhausted by then. So, we walked to a yogurt stand inside the medical center to enjoy a well-earned treat. We must have walked at least a mile, but we never once stepped foot outside. MD Anderson is seriously big.

I'll finish this post by telling a story about a woman Kim met this morning while I had my MRI. She is the wife of a man with a brain tumor. They are in their early thirties. I took note of them when they entered the waiting room, and when I got to my prep room to don the hospital garb, I said to myself, "Kim and that woman will wind up chatting the whole time." Sure enough, after the procedure was over, Kim told me that family's story and showed me a book the woman, Lilla, gave her: *The Practice of the Presence of God* by Brother Lawrence.

Kim read short letters to me from this book while we anxiously waited to get the final word on whether we'd proceed with surgery. This time was a reminder that "resting" with God is not passive; it is active and must be practiced continually to be truly experienced.

Peace.

# It's the Day Before the Day

## *April 13, 2016*

Hi folks

Well, this post is a difficult one. It's hard enough for me to write this often where I'm the primary focus, as it makes me feel awfully self-absorbed; I'd much rather come alongside others who are hurting and share their burdens. Or go fishing. But, I guess with this procedure tomorrow, I'll burden you all with some prayer requests. We humbly appreciate it. And we promise to pray now and for each of you in the years to come. Many years to come.

Back home, Kim's parents (Gaga and Gibby) are managing the household. Please pray:

For the strength of Kim's parents, Gibby in particular, as he is very ill himself with his own battle with the "little c" (cancer).

For Joy, Caroline, Samantha, and Owen, that they will have peace, love each other well, and be easy for their grandparents.

For the surgery tomorrow, please pray:

That the surgical team will have great wisdom and

skill to remove all of the cancer yet optimally pre-serve healthy tissue.

That if my bladder must be removed, the nerves and vessels in that area are preserved.

That if intraoperative radiation is necessary, it kills all cancer cells without damaging the surrounding tissue.

That the newly installed colostomy bag will be tempo-rary.

For peace and comfort for Kim, my mother (Nancy), my sister (Nan), and my father (Charlie) as they spend the day waiting at MD Anderson.

That should cover us! Thanks for all your love and support.

I'll finish with this. As I was leaving the medical cen-ter Monday afternoon, it occurred to me that I feel like I live by hope much more than I live by faith. I don't mean this in a necessarily negative way. As my broth-er/friend/pastor Jared Bryant said this morning, Paul in Corinthians 13:13 tells us that faith, hope, and love abide forever, but he mentioned that many people are geared towards one of these more than others. And for me, I live resolutely in the hope of eternity, that when the lights of this world go out, new ones turn on. I cast my sight on the horizon, which is wonderful when you can see it. But the enormity of difficult circumstances can rock you, your sight becomes limited, and even the hope of a far-off promised land may provide little solace.

I picture the scene in the movie *Alive* when Nando and Roberto are trying to escape the Andes. After two days, they reach the top of a treacherous mountain, believing the coast of Chile lies on the other side, only to see an infinity of mountains. Their hopes crushed, Nando finds some resolve from within, some strength (faith?) to persevere. And they proceed to trek an additional 12 days to rescue. Dramatized or not, the point is that hope without faith is easily turned to doubt and uncertainty. They could have turned back. I could abandon my hope and despair. But it is only by remembering that Christ is with me always that I carry on with joy and purpose now.

I'm thankful for all my friends who have such strong faith for me to rely on. Perhaps I occasionally remind them of the sweet goal of our perseverance. And together there is the love that binds us as a body. And the "big C" (I hope you know what I mean by this one) that upholds us.

Peace, love, and humble appreciation.

# Update on the Surgery

## *April 14, 2016, 11pm*

Thank you all for your prayers and support. Unfortunately, the surgery was shorter than expected. It was determined after opening me up that removing the tumor was not going to be the best course of action. Please continue to pray for peace and understanding as both Kim and I are discouraged and confused. We will know more once we speak with the surgeon tomorrow.

# The Boat

## *April 15, 2016, 4am*

*[Note: featured image removed. It depicted a brick path-way through a park of long-stand·ing hardwoods between two residential streets with homes only on the side oppo-site the park. It gives the neighborhood a calm, peaceful setting.]*

I lie here on my hospital bed. It's 4am. Painkillers and "benzos" course through my body. I await the arrival of the doctor sometime this morning to give me the news of what's next. This is the height of uncertainty.

I told my family that I feel like I've been clinging to a rope, dangling from a cliff, but the rope has many knots to which I can cling. But with every bit of bad news I slip to the next knot, and I fear for how many knots remain. I forget that it's not me clinging to a rope but Christ clinging to me.

Re-read the first two sentences of this blog and forgive me if I sound wacko.

I took the picture at the top of the page here in Hous-ton, and I just love it. The cropped version I used for this blog theme doesn't do the photograph justice, but it captures some nice metaphorical elements: there's a clear path to some unknown destination, there are woods surrounding, but on either side there are roads where cars come and go and people live.

Now imagine it's totally dark and someone has given you a pen light. And instead of a smooth, straight, cobblestone path, you can perceive that the path is windy and you can sense that danger lies ahead. You're uncertain as to whether to remain on the path or take your chances through the forest to arrive on what must be a road, given the sounds and headlights of cars. But what if I told you that awaiting you at the end of this path is something more glorious than anything you could find out in the world that surrounds us? And what if I told you that there are many people encouraging you and a Helper to guide you? Would you walk the hard road?

Sounds obvious, but it isn't. No one alive has ever seen what lies at the end of the path. There are stories, but it is a long journey to endure with such uncertainty, clinging to one big promise that was made over 2000 years ago.

I've told this story to others before, but I can't stop thinking about the image of Christ and his disciples crossing the sea of Galilee during a torrential rain storm, in Mark 4: 35-41. The disciples are experiencing this mayhem, but Jesus sleeps peacefully in the back of the boat (He's tired from all his work!). Mark says, "High waves were breaking into the boat, and it began to fill with water" (Mark 4:37, NLT). Though not written, I picture a scene of panic: some frantically bailing water, maybe a couple of disciples frozen with fear, and others attempting to rouse Jesus, shouting "Teacher, don't you care that we're going to drown?" (4:38). Jesus awakes, but I get the sense that Jesus is annoyed. He silences the storm with a word and then rebukes his disciples by asking them, "Why are you afraid? Do you still have no faith?" (4:40).

Again, picture the scene. What is "doubting" Thomas doing? Looking out at the storm and thinking it's the end? Peter, Christ's close but oft mistaken friend, shouting commands to others in order to save themselves? And perhaps John, the "disciple that Jesus loved" waiting patiently for whatever happens? I'm conjecturing mightily here.

The crazy thing is, they had Jesus with them! They'd already seen him perform many miracles, and yet there was fear and doubt. They paid more attention to the world around them and all its dangers than to Christ who was with them.

Can you relate to this? I certainly can.

I like to think of my brothers and sisters in Christ all being on a boat with me out on a sea. We celebrate the good days (there's plenty of food and sunscreen) and we cling together during the difficult times. But in those difficult moments, who or what do we put our faith in? If you're one to fixate on the problem at hand, despair may set in. If you're like me, you tend to look around you at all of the people you love and who love you and find comfort there. Maybe some will just want to jump ship. We all share, as did the disciples, these tendencies.

Because if we look in the back of the boat, there's no one there sleeping who we just need to waken to solve our problems.

But our hope and the faith that we've been given tell us that He is there. In his spirit. All around us. Not necessarily to solve our current problems, but to encourage us and remind us that our ultimate problem, that of the destinies of our souls, has already been solved. An immutable result of his death and resurrection. Praise God.

What's been most interesting about writing this blog while I battle cancer is that I'm getting comments, texts, and phone calls from so many people, many of whom, quite frankly, I wouldn't have thought were believers. They tell me they're praying for me. You want to know this person who is in complete control of the raging seas of our lives? He is listening to our prayers, is knowable in the living Bible, and desires our worship in His church.

My hope is that there are some new people in the boat with us. That the prayers they offer up have a profound effect on them. That they'll visit a local church and experience what it's like to belong to a body. As Pastor Don Aldin once said, belief and belonging go hand-in-hand. They reinforce each other.

Thanks to Pastor Rob Edwards of Mercy Presbyterian in Lynchburg, Va for his thought provoking sermon on Mark 4:35-41. If interested, I can probably provide it.

Thanks for all the love you're showing me and my family!

# What the Doctor Said

## *April 16, 2016*

Hey folks

So, this isn't necessarily easy to post, but given that I've been open with the history, I guess I need to be open with the present and future. Perhaps I was hoping that at least part of the cancer in my body was going to be "history"....

When they opened me up, they discovered what the doctor termed "seeds of cancer" on the abdominal wall, particularly on the right side of my body. I'm not really sure of the extent of it; bottom line is that the doctor didn't want to proceed with complicated surgery that might result in delayed healing and allow these seeds to grow into full-fledged tumors. That would be bad.

So, it's time for me to heal up and get back on chemo. I have a lovely incision from sternum to groin that needs to heal.

As far as future options, there is a procedure that they do here called HIPEC that might be an option down the road. And there are some other options to treat the abdomen. The pelvic area is just tricky to treat. I'll need to meet with the oncologist here to determine a treatment plan.

I can't lie. I feel defeated. But life goes on, as they say. People tell me to stay positive, but I don't really know what that means. I'm going to stay eternal. For some reason that gives me a lot more comfort.

Thanks again for all of the support and prayers. We feel so covered in love, and I know that this is strong testimony to the present reality of resurrection life. It isn't easy, but I know Christ is using this trial to transform me, Kim, my kids, and my family and friends into who we were really meant to be. When I look at pictures of myself from when I was younger, I'm struck at least as much as how I've aged physically as I have grown spiritually. And I really wouldn't wish to go back

# Hopefully Getting Out Today

## *April 18, 2016*

Greetings all.

What a difference the morning can make. What is it with the night, anyway, that can make us so uneasy? Darkness isn't inherently evil, as some might think; it's indifferent. But since God created a universe that penetrated darkness, there seems to be a real perception of separation from our Creator when we despair in the night. Christ talks a lot about darkness and light and this is something I've been thinking a lot about, but that's for another time.

Yesterday was another interesting day in "the boat." I woke up longing to be at home so I could attend our worship service at Resurrection Presbyterian in Athens. I knew that I could wait until the sermon was posted online, but I still wished to be there to fellowship, sing, pray, worship, and hear a sermon on the Gospel. I jokingly (somewhat) asked pastor Jared if they could stream it to me. He really liked the idea and endeavored to make it happen! Ultimately, we used Skype and had one of our young congregants hold up his phone so I could watch. No, I didn't sing, but being able to connect with my hometown church while sitting atop the hospital on the observation deck was an unforgettable experience. The "passing of the peace" portion of the service was particularly fun, as I got to see many loving faces while they saw my unwashed-in-four-days self in a hospital gown. Resurrection is truly a "come as you are" church.

So back to why I mentioned the darkness earlier. I must say that I'm healing very well and everyone here is very surprised and pleased by my quick progress. But there has been one issue that has been lingering that has been causing me anxiety (I'll spare you the gross details). Even though the doctors, nurses, and other care people have assured me that the issue is not uncommon and would resolve, I just haven't been able to find ease with it. My anxiety about it got so bad last night that Kim and I had to leave our room to go back to the observatory deck to pray.

(That last sentence should immediately raise a red flag, but let me continue.) It was after 9pm, and we were the only folks up there, other than a woman cleaning. Houston is being hammered by rain right now, so we sat in a quiet, low-lit area, listening and literally feeling the storm outside. The windows were bowing from the pressure of the wind and were creaking at the seals. It occurred to me that this was how I was feeling on the inside. Battered, bending, creaking. And yet safe with Christ. Kim put her small, loving hands on my belly and prayed. And then she asked me if it was "well with my soul". I paused briefly, but the answer was undoubtedly yes. It's just that the brokenness of my body and the perfection of my soul battle it out in my head to unnerve me. Especially at night.

Providentially, I found great comfort in the feeling of physical safety in this hospital from the powerful storm. And also Providentially, I found almost immediate, great comfort from the Spirit of Christ as I returned to my room. Somehow, I knew that my issue was going to resolve itself with the new day.

Returning to my struggle with anxiety: just in case it wasn't obvious, what is wrong with my statement of "it got so bad that I had to pray"? Prayer should NOT be your last resort. It is a discipline that should keep you feeling God's presence always.

On Saturday, I lovingly kicked my mom, dad, and wife out of my room so I could have a moment alone. There have not been many of these moments. I turned the lights down and was about to rest when my pain-management nurse came in to my room. Somehow, perhaps in the unspoken words we exchanged in the way we looked at each other, she ended up telling me the story about her husband's battle with cancer and how he has been disease-free for four years. She said, "God cured my husband." I won't go into the details, but she encouraged me to simply pray that "God is good. God loves me. God has a good plan for me. God will not forsake me."

As anyone who has spent time in a hospital knows, you get awoken many times during the night for medication, vital signs, blood draws, etc. Every time they woke me up last night, I said those prayers and then fell back asleep.

The words in these short prayers and their importance were not new to me as a mature believer, but the reminder to say them was critical.

I need spiritual discipline. We need spiritual discipline.

And guess what? This morning the disconcerting issue seems to be resolving. Based on what we can see and on the latest blood work (I saw the doctor at 6 am), it looks like I'll be getting out of here this afternoon.

Houston is under a flash flood warning today, so I just may need a real boat to get from the hospital to the hotel :).

# Yes, They Released Me

## *April 19, 2016*

*[Note: featured image removed. It was taken from an upper-floor of the Wyndham Hotel at the Texas Medical Center in Houston. The foreground shows the dense treetops hiding the houses in the nearby neighborhood with the Houston skyline in the distance.]*

Here's a view of my hotel room at the Wyndham. Ok, it's a suite. My mother and Kim are with me. I'm catching up on work and awaiting our first doctor's appointment tomorrow with the oncologist. Hopefully, we'll come up with a treatment plan that we can have confidence in. The appt is 2:30pm central. Appreciate your prayers, as always. We'll know more, like when we can come home, tomorrow evening, I suspect.

As I write, the End Title theme of *Shawshank Redemption* is playing. Apropro?  Who doesn't remember the words of Red at the end: "Get busy living or get busy dying..."

I removed the end of his quote for sake of younger audiences, but that IS right.

# Heading Home Saturday

## *April 21, 2016*

Hey folks,

Thanks again for all of your prayers, kind words, and support of my family. We're so very thankful for the blessing of such a selfless group of people.

We had a good meeting with our oncologist yesterday. Ultimately, it was decided that we will stay on the current treatment plan since it has been mostly effective in shrinking/keeping in remission micro-cancer and keeping stable the solid tumor(s). We won't know for sure if there will be another plan for surgery until we meet w/ the surgical oncology team and the HIPEC team on Friday.

We did leave with some bit of new hope. I can't go into any details because there really are none, but the oncologist recently returned from a conference, and he said that he had heard "rumblings of a new immunotherapy drug" for the population of people with my cancer type (considering the presence/absence of mutations in certain genes) to be presented at a big conference in June. If this is the case, then we'll be trying like mad to get on the list for a Phase 1 trial, because if these drugs work, they can have tremendous effects on disease. They stimulate the body's own immune system to destroy cancer cells with very little side effects. We can pray that this new treatment becomes available, because then maybe surgery won't be necessary at all.

But again, this is only in the "hope" phase.

So, unless my healing suddenly takes a turn for the worse, we'll be home Saturday afternoon.

Peace and love

# Not Heading Home Saturday

## *April 22, 2016*

Greetings all! Today is the 21st anniversary of our marriage. We may not be having a rom-com-like day, but we are spending it together!

We met with the surgeon this morning, and he wants me to come see him on Monday. I have one small area in my incision that continues to leak a little, and he just wants to make sure it is not getting infected. It's not bad, he just wants to be sure. They think I'll begin to heal a lot better now that the staples have been removed. So, it looks like we'll be coming home on Tuesday, instead. Sigh. I miss my family! And Cooper (dog). And Caspian a little (cat).

By the way: staple removal. KELLY CLARKSON! KELLY CLARKSON! (to quote Steve Carell's chest-waxing screams in *The 40-Year-Old Virgin*). This was beyond painful. I've had staples removed before, but with the number of clips that I had and the soreness that was there, I almost passed out.

In other news, I met with the HIPEC surgeon as well. We went into the visit expecting him to say that I wasn't a candidate so we wouldn't be disappointed. Well, not only does he consider me a candidate, he had a plan that no one had thought of. Because his work requires about 6 hours in the OR and the tumor-removal surgery is highly complicated and would take around 12 hours, his suggestion was that we do the HIPEC first, let me heal up from that, and then do the surgery to remove the primary tumors. Oh. Cool. Good idea. (that's why we're at MD Anderson.)

I then asked him his time frame, thinking that he would say around 6 months or so. Instead, he said 2-3 weeks.  That's right. 2-3 weeks. Oh my. Scary, but that actually makes sense. Get in there and treat the area before any of the newly detected disease has any time to grow.

He's going to present his idea at one of their weekly conferences. This is another benefit of these large cancer centers. Medical oncologists, radiation oncologists, surgeons, and other specialists all gather in a room, and doctors present the cases of particular individuals. They then discuss various options in order to come up with a plan that is best for the patient. He will present my case on Thursday, so we'll wait to hear what is decided.

Just another day in the boat!  Rock, rock, Jesus please make the storm stop! I'll be honest, I even got "seasick" today.

I'm so glad I'm not alone. My wife sits by my side always. As I write, my mother, Kim and I are sitting in our hotel room enjoying the blue sky and warm sun and the beautiful view of North Houston (cities always look pretty from a distance). And there is so much sweetness around the medical center. You can feel it. It brings comfort and peace. I see so many couples hand-in hand, walking the corridors, with one of those hands bearing a white patient wristband. As hard as it is to fight for your life, it really can enrich the days you have with a love that covers you. And I have this in the greatest of portions through family and friends and my church body.

My heart really aches for the people that I see that are by themselves battling cancer or going through other difficult times. Oh the groans of this broken creation. I'm sure they too find comfort in the presence of love throughout the center. But the greatest comfort is knowing that no one is really alone who puts their faith and hope in Jesus Christ. And if they do, I know there is a body of believers that will give them the love and support they need.

Self-giving love. That is a life of true purpose. Brent

# 5:08

## *April 25, 2016*

This is the departure time of our flight. We are coming home. We look forward to normal routines, except that I can't lift anything over 8 pounds or so for another 4 weeks.

I hope to catch up with everyone soon.

Humble thanks for your support.

Brent

# Remembering...

## *April 26, 2016*

The doctor says, "this is the best course of action based on what we know now."

We are fighting at least three battle fronts. Twelve days ago there were two. There is cancer in the sewer of my body. There is cancer in the network of lymph nodes that is meant to protect me. And we learned from the originally cancelled and last week aborted surgery to remove the tumors of the sewer that there is disease hiding out in my pelvis too. It is the realization of your greatest fear that you are up against guerrilla warfare from an indifferent enemy; you plot attacks, corral defenses, but yet you can only plan from your current purview against a completely unpredictable adversary.

So, the doctors can only make decisions about the current circumstances. The outcomes follow directly from these decisions. There's no way to know if a different treatment plan would result in a better outcome due to a yet unforeseen factor. And this is how life operates. It generates a timeline of events.

But can you imagine the Creator of the universe operating this way? Always intervening at the desires of his people who believe they know what is best for them?  But God happens to know all unforeseen factors, so His good path for us may be (and likely is) vastly different from what we believe and what we pray for. As we continue to pray for each other, we always end with a "thy will be done" because we know and trust that God's will is best.

But we continue to pray for people's sufferings to end!  For the lonely to find companionship, those struggling financially to find a stable job, for those with addictions to be freed, those struggling with depression to experience joy, those enduring difficult relationships to see reconciliation, and those fighting disease to discover a miracle cure. But the reality is that these difficulties are meant to transform us. Meant to help us know this triune God that loves us. He loves us so much that His Son was crucified for us.

Coming home has been more difficult than I expected. First, I certainly haven't come home with the feeling of a victor from a battle but simply battered from the fight. Then, there is coming home to the bills that have been waiting for me and some bits of bad news--all before lunch. And then there's the looming uncertainty of the next steps.

BUT I AM HERE. I HAVE A WONDERFUL FAMILY. WONDERFUL CHURCH. WONDERFUL FRIENDS. WONDERFUL JOB. I AM TRULY BLESSED.

I AM NOT FORSAKEN!

Reminding myself of these truths doesn't necessarily remove the feeling that they are lies, though. In my selfishness, with all the blessings in my life, I still have the nerve to ask, "God, why won't you bless me in *these* ways?" I confess fearing that God's will may take me further down a path of suffering, and I will resist letting go of the comfortable life that I envision instead of embracing the enriched life that he is revealing.

A lot of my frustration is that I feel called to serve. I want so much to see our church, Resurrection Presbyterian, grow and build its own brick-and-mortar home on the East Side of Athens. I want to see people moving towards one another, building community, experiencing fellowship with one another and with God. I want to see His Kingdom grow. I want to see His work in everything and have infinite reasons to praise Him.

But right now, I'm not praising. I'm simply trying to remember. And God has been providing so many sovereign "coincidences" (signs) that he is with me and at work.

For some reason, I thought of the movie *Field of Dreams*. Ray (Kevin Costner) hears voices that encourage him to build a baseball field in his corn field. He then hears voices and experiences "coincidences" (again, signs) that lead him to travel around the country meeting different people that are somehow connected to his story. They all end up at his farm in Iowa playing baseball with spirits (or ghosts) of the 1919 Chicago White Sox, with "Shoeless" Joe Jackson being the primary character.

I'm sure many of you know the story. If you don't, then you should see it.

Towards the end, the living people that he has brought to Iowa are invited to join the ghosts to leave the baseball field and enter the corn from whence the White Sox players have come. There is some mystical destination in the corn. When Ray finds that he is not invited, he is indignant. He's worked so hard, but, yet, he doesn't know his part in the story. He finally asks Shoeless Joe, "what's in it for me?", to which Joe, if memory serves, says "you better stay here, Ray." Joe then leaves the field to disappear with the others into the corn.

Ray is left to himself, confused. But then he sees one remaining player out in the field. And he walks out there to join him in a game of catch. It's Ray's father, with whom he was estranged in life and regretted not knowing better. What Ray was meant to get out of this was the ability to meet his father.

What I'm meant to get out of all of this is to meet my Heavenly Father. I will know Him more and more as He supports me through difficult days and the rejoicing moments of sharing love with family and friends. We each can share a moment in time, yes, but in dark days and light, with glory always on the horizon, even a simple hug between believers can be a powerful reminder of the sweetness of Christ's love to be shared for all eternity. A fool's dream to some, an absolute truth to others, and perhaps a shaky hope for those with whom God is still cultivating a mustard seed of faith.

So, on days like these, when I'm feeling awfully discouraged, my wife reminds me to remember my blessings. It's no different from when the grumbling Israelites were stranded in the desert after fleeing Egypt; they were encouraged to remember the Passover. Remembering what God has done for us provides the encouragement to persevere.

Remember, remember, remember. New days equal new mercies. New mercies provide new remembrances. This is how we meet our Father.

# Fast Current

## *April 29, 2016*

Hello all.

I again want to humbly thank you for your love and support of me and my family. I also want to thank you for all of the kind words to me personally. "Blogging" (or whatever this is) is obviously uncharted water for me (I promise I'll quit the watery metaphors very soon), but your encouragement has given me the confidence to continue. And we're going to continue to need your support as we move forward in quickly changing and uncertain circumstances. And please, send me your prayer requests, too! We would love to share your burdens with you. And your praises.

Yesterday was supposed to be the day that we found out what the immediate next steps are. You may recall that we met with a doctor that performs a procedure called HIPEC for which he thinks I'm a good candidate. The only question is when to perform it. On Thursday mornings, groups of doctors (and presumably researchers) get together to discuss various patient cases. Our new doctor was to present my case to his committee so that they could collectively determine what treatment plan is best for me.

Well, as it turns out, there was a larger conference going on, so their committee did not meet. So, our case will be presented next Thursday. However, in order to not lose any time in case they DO want to proceed with HIPEC, a physician's assistant called me yesterday to discuss possible surgery dates. She informed me that there was only 1 day available until July and that it took her over 3 hours of schedule shifting between different groups to get this date. And that day is May 9. Egad!

I suppose that if this is going to happen, it is best that it happens soon, both from a cancer-fighting standpoint but also so I don't have more days to dwell on these things. Next Wednesday, we will fly out to Houston, spend the night, and wake up to meet with the doctor. It will be good to meet face-to-face to have him explain what the committee recommends. If we're a go for HIPEC, we will then meet with the appropriate groups to sign consents. Regardless, we'll be returning Thursday afternoon, so we can spend the weekend with family. We'll fly back out on Sunday the 8th if I'm to have surgery.

This is all I know for now.

Before I continue, I want to be clear about something. I hope you don't read what follows as complaining. As I've told many people, I feel so strangely fortunate to be a part of what I perceive as God at work. There's a whole lot going on around us beyond just what is happening in my family, and God has given us the opportunity to continue to be a part of His work. Just a mere glimpse of it is nourishment to carry on; He's provided the desire, the peace, the strength, and the endurance to do so. I mean, what else can it be? Otherwise, I think I'd be losing my mind. Or I've already lost it and just don't realize it.

Believe it or not, I'm actually working. I have my "mobile workstation" with me, trying to do what I get paid to do. But as I write this entry, there are people in my house hanging shutters (Kim wanted them and what are we waiting for?), there is paperwork in my Inbox for me to sign so I can refinance my house, and it's Friday, which means "can so-and-so spend the night, etc" when the kids get home. All the while, my dear mother is making travel arrangements for us to go to Houston next week and we (more like Kim) begin to think about what we're going to do if we are going to be out of town for several weeks. Sadly, we heard yesterday that Kim's father, also a cancer survivor, will spend next week in the hospital to fight pneumonia. And yet this morning, I heard some extraordinarily encouraging news concerning some dear friends -- praiseworthy news for which we've been praying for a long time.

The point is that today is just another day in the life of a believer. We have all of the usual typical and the difficult stuff, but we also have the promise that none of these moments are fleeting, that all we do has purpose and should be for God's glory. In and through our daily affairs there seems to be a current of otherworldly energy binding it all together and moving lives forward. We are gifted with the opportunity to participate in Christ's redemption of the world. And while God doesn't rely on us to accomplish His goals, it is in our labors that He loves us, teaches us, and feeds us with His grace.

So, while I'm happy that I'll be saving money from refinancing and also improving my earthly home, it is the promise of the treasures being stored up for us in our Heavenly home (Mat 6:19-20) that really makes this life worth living. And worth fighting for.

Peace and love,

Brent

# One Flew Over the Cuckoos Nest

## *May 4, 2016*

Greetings folks

I hope this post finds you well. Kim and I continue to be covered in support and love, both physically and spiritually. Thank you to all those who provide meals, treat our kids as your own, visit us, and pray for us. We continue to thank God for all of you and pray that He fills you with the love and peace of the Spirit of his Son.

Kim and I leave today for Houston for a 1-day visit. We'll spend the night at the Rotary House, a hotel which adjoins MD Anderson. Thursday morning from 7:30-8:30, the newest member of our medical team will meet with a group of other doctors and present my case. As I've said, our new doctor's plan is to perform the HIPEC surgery on May 9, but he wants medical oncologists and others to weigh in on what they think is the best strategy. Most likely, the options are to perform the HIPEC surgery immediately or for me to start back on systemic chemotherapy and hope to perform the necessary surgical procedures down the road.

This is the first time in our battle where I honestly don't

know what I think is best for me in terms of treatment. In the past, I've been asked for very specific prayer requests. I certainly appreciate this because people want to know how to pray for others. I want to know how best to pray for others. But in this case, I don't know if it is best for me to have HIPEC surgery on Monday and then spend 3-4 weeks in the hospital. Don't get me wrong, this sounds like a great plan and really is the only option now to attempt to kill metastatic cancer cells in my gut. The scary thing is knowing that I will need to be off chemo for a longer time, thus giving cancer cells in my lymphatic system the chance to grow into solid tumors. And then there is the disease of the "sewer system" that we had attempted to remove 3 weeks ago that would also be given the opportunity to grow.

So, I think it best to pray that the doctors have the wisdom to decide the best course of action for me and that I will have peace with whatever decision they make. And please pray for our kids as they get shuttled around to different families while we are in Houston. If HIPEC is the next step, our little kiddies are going to have their lives quite disrupted right at the end of the school year.

I should tell you that I feel peace. I'm not dreading this trip, and I don't feel fear about what the doctors are going to say. I hope this is the "peace that surpasses all understanding" (Philippians 4:7) and not a worldly sort of resignation. It feels like the former. I've felt resignation, and this seems different.

Looking back, visits with doctors seem to reveal which life my heart is clinging to: the life I want and the life God has given me. I often think of the interaction between stuttering Billy Bibbit and indifferent but controlling Nurse Ratched in the movie *One Flew Over the Cuckoo's Nest*. Towards the end, Billy finally experiences a moment of confidence and a spirit of freedom, only to have that spirit shoved back into its prison by Nurse Ratched, to see the return of the stuttering Billy that belongs under her control (if you are an adult, you can YouTube "Billy Bibbit Scene"). For me, freedom is in trusting God with my life – there is real peace there. But I want to find security in science and medicine. There are promises there, but prognoses are clinical and capricious. And negative ones can feel like a prison sentence. One moment you may feel alive, assured, and the next minute the blood drains from your face, anxiety overtakes you, and no words about hope provide comfort. Nurse Ratched glares at you in cold victory. This has happened so many times.

When I had my first surgery back in 2013, I wrote on a bit of stationary the following verse, and taped it to my hospital gurney (Psalm 112:6-8, NIV): "[6] Surely the righteous will never be shaken; they will be remembered forever. [7] They will have no fear of bad news; their hearts are steadfast, trusting in the Lord. [8] Their hearts

**70**

are secure, they will have no fear; in the end they will look in triumph on their foes." I want so much for this to be true, that I will have no fear and that ultimately we will triumph over our foe, which to me is cancer. Honestly, I have to admit that I have always feared bad news. But I do NOT fear that I won't see triumph; I know I will see triumph in the gift of eternal fellowship with God. It's just that I fear that the foe that must be defeated is not really the cancer but my sin of wanting absolute control over my life.

So, as I am asked for and then provide ever-simplifying prayer requests, I sense my grip on this life weakening. Not in a defeated way but in a victorious way. As I let go of the life that I want and feel I deserve, I am energized by the eternal life I have been given. It is ever-present. Available to all. Visible with eyes to see. Attainable to vulnerable hearts.

If I see you, don't be surprised if I hug you firmly. I will cling to the eternal bond between us. With all of this support, I am filled with a peace that will fear no bad news.

# Shawshank

## *May 5, 2016*

I don't know why I communicate with movie meta-phors. I was an English major a long time ago and you'd think I'd have literary references to use. But for some reason movie scenes just come to mind. Perhaps be-cause they're visual.

Anyway, imagine the scene in *Shawshank Redemption*. Andy Dufresne is crawling through a sewage pipe and a heavy storm booms outside. The music builds. He wretches frequently but he perseveres. Ultimately, nearly exhausted, he sees light, trudges on and falls into a river to wash away the filth of Shawshank prison. He stands, raises his face and arms high, lets the rain fall on him, and exalts in triumph. In redemption?

But consider this non-Hollywood possibility: for all of Andy's planning of his escape, for all of his years of scraping away at his cell wall and outwitting his cap-tors by hiding his rock hammer in his Bible, what would he have done had there been bars blocking the end of that pipe? I realize the ending of the movie would have stunk (literally), but wouldn't it have made sense to put some kind of barrier there to prevent animals or some fool from crawling INTO the prison? Can you imagine

Andy reaching another set of prison bars mere meters from freedom?

Cut!

If we're honest, we all imagine paths through difficultly to happiness. Something like: "life would be good if ......"

You know what I would write there.

Before I walked into the doctor's office this morning, I bowed my head to pray. Mindfully resting in a Holy peace, His spirit reminded me that He already knew what the doctors had decided. For me, that decision had been made that morning and I was waiting to hear it. To the eternal God of the universe it is a footfall on the path that he would have me follow.

Psalm 25:4 says "Show me the right path, O Lord, point out the road for me to follow". (NLT)

The doctors have told me that surgery is not a good idea at this time. I need to go back on systemic chemo-therapy. There appears no medical path to cure.

I asked Kim what God might be trying to say today. She said, "God is still working on us." Amen. The doctors' decision is not indicative of having hiked a tough trail only to reach a sign that says not only is there no end but also no return. The paths are always unfolding. I can choose now to stop believing that God has a good plan for me and trek out into the wilderness on my own. Or I can heed the encouragement of family and friends, continue to trust God, and step into the unknown in faith.

But in the midst of a thicket, how do I know I'm on a path? Especially the right one that God points out to me? In these times of struggle, both physically and spiritually, and as I attempt to write honestly about the difficulties of following Christ, my phone rings with comments, texts, and emails that all tell me that God is clearly at work. That my faith is apparent.

I hope you see that this is not of my own making. Only by His grace can my despair be read as hope. I pray that God is being glorified.

So, we fight on. The good news is that I haven't "ruined summer" (assuming the thoughts of my kids) by being in a hospital hundreds of miles away or recovering from surgery and not being any fun. Cancer science continues and the possibility of new therapies for my cancer type are on the horizon. But I can't allow myself to traverse a path that such treatments might promise. This is only a recipe for disappointment.

Redemption is not at the end of the journey but now and ongoing. So I endeavor to stay in the moment. To be thankful. Hoping and striving to be of use. Face set not on a path that I envision but lifted to feel the soft rain of God's daily mercy. Trusting that His hand is guiding me. My wife's hand reminding me of His love.

# *Season 2*

## *Chemotherapy & the Dark Night of the Soul*

*It is now a month since the failed surgery, and I have resumed FOLFIRI chemotherapy. Suffice to say, my body is still healing. In fact, the incision near my belly-button had opened, and my wife had to help me clean it and pack it with gauze until it closed. I think this period is aptly titled "Dark Night of the Soul," because of the wrestling with faith that ensued (Dark Night of the Soul was a poem by a 16th century Spanish poet, thank you Pastor Aldin). Keep in mind I was under the influence of a lot of heavy drugs and probably a bit depressed, but the period was extraordinarily transformative. Without the near constant health-related activities, I began to explore more deeply faith-related topics.*

# Of Books and Containers, Part I

## *May 9, 2016*

Greetings all,

Now that I'm settling into a routine of chemo, there won't be much "hot" news about my cancer battle from a physical standpoint. What follows is an entry about my spiritual journey (battle seems an inappropriate word).

Well, it has been almost 4 weeks since the surgery, and I continue to heal up. I haven't healed as quickly as from previous surgeries, probably because this was the most intrusive, even though the "major" part of the surgery was aborted. Soon I'll get back on systemic chemotherapy. The doctors want me on chemo for 3 months and then get new scans. I admit that I feel myself grieving the fact that surgery is not an option, at least not yet. But my kids say that they're happy that I didn't have surgery. They were scared and just want us all at home. I understand that. And interestingly, whenever I've told folks "no surgery" I hear a congratulatory response. They think that this must obviously mean good news. I won't remind people that I really need surgery to remove some of the advanced disease. Who knows, maybe this is good news?

In my 14 years of being a member of a PCA church, we have often talked about how God works through ordinary and extraordinary means. This may be the same language used in other churches, but I don't know. Regardless, ordinary means are the things of this world working as we expect or hope, and God can influence these means according to His will. We might notice this influence as "coincidence" or as uncertain circumstances resolving with positive outcomes against improbable odds. We praise God for these moments.

Extraordinary means are a little tricky. All of creation must follow the natural laws of the universe, otherwise we'd have chaos. But when something happens that is totally unexplainable, we cry miracle and really bring the praises. Hosannas. Each of us probably has a miraculous story to tell, of personal experience or shared by another.

Yesterday morning I spent time in prayer before church. I first praised God for who He is and for His blessings to me. I thanked him for his son, Jesus, who died on the cross for my sins and shares His resurrection with me. I then prayed for family and friends, for peace and positive outcomes of difficult circumstances. Finally, I considered my current situation. I thanked the Lord for the people praying for me and my family. I certainly want the positive outcome to my cancer battle for which these warriors are praying. But, in the stream of thoughts coming from prayer, flowing from my mind came something like, "We are running out of ordinary means with which to fight cancer. If I'm going to beat this thing, you'll have to use extraordinary means."

(Hand slaps head) – Did I really just pray that?

Fortunately, when I was finished, Kim read for me yesterday's daily devotional from Paul David Tripp's *New Morning Mercies.* This book really is amazing, and whenever Kim reads to me, it seems just what I need to hear. I think that's because it's truth. Anyway, the devotional was on "daily bread." He referenced 1 Kings 17: 8-16, the story of the widow of Zeraphath, where Elijah visits a poor woman and asks for water and bread in the midst of an extreme drought. The distraught woman tells him, "I have nothing baked, only a handful of flour in a jar and a little oil in a jug. And now I am gathering a couple of sticks that I may go in and prepare it for myself and my son, that we may eat it and die" (1 Kings 17:12, ESV). Elijah responds by telling her to not fear, but to first make him a cake because "for thus says the Lord, the God of Israel, 'The jar of flour shall not be spent, and the jug of oil shall not be empty, until the day that the Lord sends rain upon the earth'" (1 Kings 17:14).

The Lord always provides. You see this over and over. The jar is always filled for God's purposes. The ram from the bushes when Abraham brought Isaac to

Moriah (Genesis 22:13). Aaron and Hur holding up Moses' exhausted arms in order to defeat the Amelekites (Exodus 17:12). Joshua leading the Israelites against the seemingly impenetrable city of Jericho (Joshua 6). The woman who is healed from disease by touching Jesus' cloak in a crowd (Luke 8:43-48). Jesus' disciples feeding 5000 people with 5 loaves of bread and 2 fish (Matthew 14:13-21). It is important to note that in all cases, God is providing for people who act by faith despite limited resources. Yes, it is Jesus' miracle to feed the 5000, but it is through his disciples, to whom He says, "they need not go away; you give them something to eat" (Mat 14:16). We act in faith and God provides. We may have limited ordinary means, but God replenishes them extraordinarily.

As I consider this, I then think of my days left on this earth. They may be few or many, I may be sick or well, but I can serve with the gifts He has given me in whatever capacity I am able. God is always working miracles through His broken people who are poor in spirit, and suffering certainly makes me thus. Void of hope in ordinary things. But this is where His mercy is felt and where it pours out into His world. This is how His kingdom comes. If I treasure the very limited ordinary things of this world, even the medicines and treatments that we hope can heal, I will be unable to give of myself for the sake of God's kingdom nor witness the extraordinary blessing of seeing Him at work.

And as to my options for fighting this disease, with God there's always hope. This is why we pray.

> *Lord, I come to you weary and heavy laden. I confess that I want my jar filled with items of comfort and ease. I'm scared to rely on you, to give up my trust in ordinary means. But in your love for us, you gave to your Son the cup of man, empty of any means to overcome our brokenness. Jesus, in your death you filled it with your blood, a now limitless font of mercy. The most extraordinary of means. As I am made poor in spirit for your sake, please strengthen me to persevere. Provide for me that I may love and serve others. Heal me that I may praise you the many days of a long life. Let my comfort be the peace of knowing that I am rich in grace. Amen.*

# Of Books and Containers, Part II

## *May 11, 2016*

As the title of my previous post promised, this is part II of my thoughts on biblical "books and containers". And in my previous post, there was no mention of any books, but there was of a container: the cup of Jesus. I want to explore this image a bit more.

In my very personal prayer at the end of my previous post, I referred to "the cup of man" that Jesus took up. Metaphorically speaking and tying the imagery of Jesus' cup to that of the widow's jar of little flour which "shall not be spent," I described the cup of man being filled with the blood of Jesus, the most extraordinary of means through which God extends His unlimited mercy.

I didn't make this cup up, though. Jesus, in his prayer to God in Gethsemane just prior to his capture and crucifixion, cries out "My Father, if it be possible, let this cup pass from me; nevertheless, not as I will, but as you will" (Matthew 26:39, ESV). But what really is in this cup? Most scholars agree that it is the cup of God's wrath. But few want to talk about God's wrath. I avoided it by saying that the cup was "empty of any means to overcome our brokenness". If the cup was filled with God's wrath, then what I said is certainly true, but there remains this issue of God's wrath. And why Jesus had to die. There is plenty to read on this subject, and I'm not going to undertake a deep discussion of wrath and grace in a blog post. But I like to explore imagery, so that's where I'm going.

Consider human wrath. It is scary. A source of great violence. Now consider the wrath of your Creator, with sovereign, indomitable will. The power to make and unmake. Frightening, right? Even for Christians. So much so, that morality is often substituted for the self-giving love that Jesus modeled for us. Why? Well, the bible talks often about God keeping a record of our lives. In the Old Testament and the New. Paul puts it succinctly, "So then each of us will give an account of himself to God." (Romans 14:12, ESV). It is deeply un-nerving to think that God is keeping track of all of my actions, especially the ones I regret. So, the Christian's temptation is to either earn God's favor by our good deeds or to avoid God's wrath by not committing acts of which we believe He disapproves. We become ves-sels of self-righteousness and hate. And for the non-believer? I suppose indifference.

In my semi-regular (while intended, I can't honestly say daily) reading of the bible, I came to Psalm 56 a couple of days ago. And here David says something beautiful and somewhat puzzling: "You keep track of all my sorrows. You have collected all my tears in your bottle. You have recorded each one in your book." (I like the NLT translation of this). While the thought of God recording all of my sins for which I will have to make an account is troubling, it is deeply encouraging to think that God remembers all of my sorrow. This sorrow could be from the trials of this life, but I think also from the effects of sin, both from the worldly consequences of it but also from the relief of guilt when we repent and are forgiven.

I offer up another story. Those concerned with orthodoxy might raise an eyebrow at what I'm about to say, but I want to share what I imagined. Just like I would with a movie. The New Testament describes a scene of a "woman of the city" (or harlot) where "standing behind him [Jesus] at his feet, weeping, she began to wet his feet with her tears and wiped them with the hair of her head and kissed his feet and anointed them with the ointment." When I thought about my tears being collected in a bottle, I thought about this woman crying on Jesus' feet and wiping them away. There's something mystical to this act. I envision this woman's tears cleansing Jesus' feet of dirt, in some way cleansing them of the corruption of the world, something that only affected his body, since His soul was pure, without sin. Through these same feet spikes would be hammered in order to hang Him on a cross. Expanded further, we have the image of Him taking this woman's tears to the cross. I then have the image of *my* tears being poured out on Him and taken to the cross, too. And here is my hope.

My pastor/brother in Christ Jared and I are attempting to memorize Psalm 25. On this particular morning, I was up to verses 1-6, but I decided to add verse 7. So, as I tossed these ideas around in my head, I read Psalm 25:7 (NLT): "Remember not the sins of my youth or my transgressions; according to your steadfast love remember me, for the sake of your goodness, O Lord!" I remember that, as a Christian, I need not fear God's wrath. When He looks at the record of my life, yes, he sees my actions, both "good" and "bad", but he sees my sorrows, knows the tears I've cried, has been with me those dark nights alone when the fear of the ultimate side effect of cancer (death) grips me. But when I stand before Him to give an account, I will fall on my knees and just thank Him for Jesus. The account of His life becomes the account of my life. When he remembers me according to his steadfast love, He will remember me in the manifestation of His love, Christ Jesus. My life taken by Him through death on a cross, resurrection, and then glorification.

Such peace and comfort here despite the groans of my body. I wish this for you all.

# Zeal Addiction

## *May 19, 2016*

I've discovered that I'm a zeal junkie.

This is how this blog came into being. My life has pretty much been on 3-month cycles. I get a CT Scan, PET Scan, MRI, bloodwork, etc, see a doctor, and then decide next steps. Repeat. Since 2014 when we discovered the recurrence, the next step has continued to be systemic chemotherapy. But every 3 months I have seen a surgeon, too, and we've kept surgical options open. Yes, we even attempted one back in April. The point is, doctor's visits, scans, and other tests agitate me. But this also energizes me. Makes me really see my need for Jesus. And then I start talking to my wife. Sometimes with agony and accompanied by tears, she would sit there, hold my hand (or my head) and listen to me narrate a journey to the deepest parts of the universe in my mind. The imagination of the realm of God, his people, his work, and what I'm supposed to be doing in it.

Heavy stuff. At least I'm thinking it is. And she tells me to write. My lifelong dream has been to write, to be honest. I just never had a vision for what it looked like professionally. Battling cancer gives you plenty to write about. But so does following Jesus earnestly.

So here I am. Post-surgery. Healing. Awaiting a new round of chemo. And, not that there aren't many needs of family and friends, it just seems that some of the most urgent issues are in a positive motion. Like we've been with God as He pushed a huge boulder up a hill and now we just get to watch it roll down the other side. I picture Forrest Gump when he abruptly stopped running. He merely said, "I think I'll go home now" and that was it. That accurately describes my feeling in the clinic when the doctor told us surgery was not a good option now. Urgency waned. And slowly, the accompanying inspiration and zeal has returned to a more every-day mode.

But I miss that feeling of zeal!

Carrying on, I started to write something last week but didn't like it. I dumped it.

Then night-before-last, I woke up in the middle of the night and pronounced, "Some people seek security. Some people seek freedom. But regardless, we are all created!"

Yes! The zeal I seek! And I was fortunate to remember the revelation in the morning. So, I prayed, meditated, and wrote. But what I found I was doing was trying to come up with some wisdom to make sense of my midnight ramblings (kudos Mick Jagger). I honestly have no idea what I was dreaming about when I awoke and screamed those words. In some vague way, I under-stand them and see their significance, but until they fit into a larger narrative, I'll leave it as a humorous story. Contrary to what my friend John suggested (jokingly), a prophet had not spoken. So those words remain an unpublished draft.

I wonder, what must it have been like for Moses? To be set apart from birth and a special instrument of God's will for your entire life. The book of Exodus de-scribes the many extraordinary ways in which God re-vealed himself to Moses in order to help Moses lead his people. We have the story of the burning bush. The cloud around Mt Sinai and the revelation of the ten commandments. Moses' staff becoming a snake at the Lord's command before Pharaoh. Moses part-ing the Red Sea. And more. I can only imagine the feel-ing of God's Presence burning inside you at moments like these. I *think* I relate to this in a very small way in times of suffering. God, of course, meets our needs. But I only imagine that His Presence ebbs and flows with my passions.

Nonetheless, as I rest in this time of healing, perhaps of recharging, emotionally I miss the Presence of God and the zeal of purpose. And yet, I have the most unusual sense of peace. Honestly. Don't misunderstand me. My body still reminds me that I have a disease. And my mind can still wander away from the comforting view of the cross. But where I think I should feel depressed about the state of my disease, I sense peace. Where I think I should act in desperation because life is fleeting, I sense patience. Where I think I should feel guilty about a lack of usefulness, I sense contentment. These are strange feelings and are markedly different from those of previous phases of this battle. It's as if I'm having a mid-life crisis while quietly passing away at the end of a long life. There's urgency. And peace.

But isn't this what it means to follow Christ? Isn't this what we hope and pray for? The crucifixion of Christ was not just an historical event 2 millennia past. His death and resurrection had saving power for people then and has it now and will until His promised return. There's urgency for people to come to faith. For his kingdom to come. But there's the peace that God is in control and that the outcome of His work is settled. That His kingdom will come.

My perception that I'm in a vacuum of God's presence is merely imagined. God was with me in the hospital at MD Anderson when I rocked about in the boat in heavy seas. And He's with me now as I may drift a bit. So rather than get anxious about a dead calm, I should cast my eyes to the horizon and enjoy the movement of the sun slowly arching in its glorious, predictable path. Feel assured. Be thankful. Wait.

God bless.

# Conspiracy Theory

## *May 23, 2016*

When you're battling cancer, you hear a lot of advice and commentary. Most of this is not coming from doctors, and I have to hope that my health team is doing their best to prolong my life, provide me with the best quality of life possible, and inform me of available options when the time is appropriate.

But there's a theory out there that the medical community ultimately doesn't want to cure people of cancer because the treatment of patients is so lucrative. I find this to be dark and difficult to believe. But there are certainly many, many clinics around the world designed to administer chemotherapy. And if cures begin proliferating, these centers would have to downsize or close. But, dear Lord, that would be glorious.

I can't help but think of another conspiracy, one that really isn't talked about, especially among believers. It is the conspiracy that God really isn't involved in our lives and that the Holy Spirit is certainly not at work to transform us. Sunday after Sunday, those of us who claim to follow Christ attend church services. Singing, praying, worshipping, even taking communion, all while carrying burdens that we pray would be lifted or that we'd be strengthened to bear. But how many of us feel stuck? Going through the motions? No change has occurred. Secretly we close our hearts, stop imagining a fulfilling future, and just be. Effectively hopeless.

As I sit in this clinic, called the "living" room, receiving toxic chemicals meant to kill cancer, I glance periodically at the bells sitting on the counter at the nurse's station. There's supposed to be hope there. If your treatment schedule has an endpoint or you receive a series of scans showing no signs of cancer, you can pick up the bell and ring it. Not only is this cathartic for the individual, but it is also meant to be an encouragement to patients in the room still fighting. That there's hope.

I've seen people ring the bell, and I confess to feeling skeptical. Though happy and hopeful for the person ringing it, I'm hesitant to believe that I can one day be free of this disease.

I've even rung the bell. Twice. The first was back in 2013 after finishing my first round of chemo. I can tell you that I definitely shook that bell halfheartedly. And last summer, after finishing 6 weeks of radiation at MD Anderson in Houston, I rang the bell with vigor. Anger. Wanting cancer to die.

Unfortunately, in both cases, I've found myself back in the clinic receiving chemo, continuing to fight. Was I ringing the bell in vain?

These bell-ringing events have reinforced the conspiracy. Not the one that says the medical field really doesn't want to cure cancer, but the one that says the gospel is not what it promises. That I should put my hope in the things of this world, the things I can see and touch, even good things, like cancer drugs. Ultimately, that the message we hear on Sundays is not about the source of life but merely good motivation for the new week, that the solutions to our problems are found elsewhere.

But rather than hoping for quick fixes or just resignedly carrying-on, seeing heaven as the consolation prize for enduring a life of suffering, I need to remember and ring often the bell that celebrates the good work that God has done in me today.

I woke up yesterday feeling angry. Ill-prepared to worship God, not wanting to listen to any "good news".  But I went for a walk and prayed. I turned my anger over to the Lord. He brought me the peace inside I sought, but, also, He inspired me to find a way to love someone a bit more that day. To do whatever I did to His glory. In my mind, I rang a bell. The day then seemed to have intensity and purpose. The worship service felt alive. A time to ring the bell. And that afternoon, I had a time of fellowship with some dear friends. Though there was heaviness to this time, I left encouraged. Renewed. A time to ring the bell. That evening, a large group gathered for dinner to say goodbye to friends who were moving away. Bittersweet, but a time to ring the bell. And the last waking act of my day was to hear my wife praying for us as we lay in bed. A time to ring the bell.

We've got to stop living life like we're trudging through some wilderness with no direction, hoping to find freedom, or even ourselves. We must recognize the small moments, the opportunities, where God continues to heal our hearts as we live out this life together. We've got to live life in the moment, as if a bell is always in our hands waiting to be rung as we doggedly refuse to accept the conspiracy that there really is no hope. We've got to give our lives over to God that we may feel the peace He provides in the reassurance that, through his Son, we are already cured of our brokenness.

Imagine the clamor of bells ringing together when a herald proclaims that God's work of redemption is complete.

> "So be truly glad. There is wonderful joy ahead, even though you must endure many trials for a little while. These trials will show that your faith is genuine. It is being tested as fire tests and purifies gold—though your faith is far more precious than mere gold. So when your faith remains strong through many trials, it will bring you much praise and glory and honor on the day when Jesus Christ is revealed to the whole world." 1 Peter: 6-7, NLT

# Ruach

## *June 8, 2016*

It was exactly a year ago that I started experiencing symptoms related to the growth of the recurrent tumor above my rectum (no use sugar-coating that). I remember this clearly because we just returned from our yearly Hilton Head vacation, and it was last year's vacation when I was experiencing extreme bloating and abdominal discomfort. Assuming that it was stress or IBS, my wife read online about how to naturally calm these symptoms, and she read about breathing techniques. You breathe in deeply through your nose, hold your breath for a moment, and then exhale slowly through your mouth. Then repeat this process. Slowly the bloating and cramping will dissipate. Along with the help of simethicone.

It's funny that proper breathing would be therapy for an ailment because as long as I've known my wife she's actually had to encourage me to breathe. For some reason, I tend to hold my breath. I can remember when we were still dating, and we would sit together watching a movie and suddenly she would say to me "breathe."  I didn't know it, but I was holding my breath.

Unfortunately, proper breathing techniques weren't enough to alleviate the problems I was having last year. As I've said before, I eventually wound up in the emergency room in Athens and had a CT scan which revealed that the tumor was nearly blocking my colon. The doctors wanted to do an emergency surgery then, but since I have been under the care of doctors at MD Anderson in Houston, they released me and put me on a liquid diet.

This all happened the week before Kim and I were to travel to Berlin, me for a conference, Kim for some good sightseeing, but instead we ended up in Houston. Again. And the doctors diverted my colon with an ostomy to save my life from the blockage, which then eliminated the bloating and pain.

I bring this story up because it relates to my breathing issues. The first night in the hospital, an alarm kept going off as I tried to sleep that was alerting the nurses that I had stopped breathing. The alarm would wake me, they'd rush in and check on me, and I got pretty annoyed and snippy. It's difficult to tell a nurse in the middle of the night that it is totally normal for me to pause when I breathe and to leave me alone. Fortunately, they removed the oxygen and the alarm the next day.

So, breathing. The simplest of things. Involuntary. But requiring discipline to perform correctly?

Last week at Hilton Head I was craving the presence of God. I just wanted to be near to Him, to feel peace. I realized that I was not going to be having regular morning devotionals and was okay with that. I wanted to focus on just being thankful to be at the beach spending time with family, simply enjoying life. And this is absolutely appropriate. To be thankful and to live for His Glory, even in the simplest of things, is to be near to Him. So, as I walked the beach, spent time with my kids and in-laws, played wiffle ball, swam in the ocean, read a book, and, yes, even enjoyed an adult beverage, I sought to do so to God's glory. I truly prayed for God to help me to glorify Him in how I did these things. These actions aren't evidently worshipful, but doing them in humble thankfulness for the blessing of such simple activities is honoring to our Creator.

But the vacation ended and then it was back to the reality of the vinyl recliner in the clinic on Monday to receive intravenous drugs which are meant to kill cancer and prolong my life. These drugs have immediate side effects, and they can make my mind go batty; sometimes with extremely hopeful thoughts but also into dark places.

Jared came to visit Kim and me, and, if I sat quietly, I could listen to them talk about "normal" stuff. But my mind tends towards "ultimate realities", as Pastor Aldin calls them, and to my interjections into their small talk, Jared would just look at me. And look at me. He'd look at me.

"Jared, what are you thinking?"

"Maybe you should just rest."

They both wanted me to rest.

Sadly, right as we were about to leave, one of the nurses reported to me that a man that I had met in the treatment room but had not seen in a while had passed away. Darkness.

Resting when you've been given a cocktail of drugs that includes steroids is easier said than done, so as Kim drove me home, I continued to talk. We passed by a cemetery and I nonchalantly asked Kim what it would be like if they had pre-dug pits for those who are just ready to die. You could fall into one, and the gravediggers would amble out with shovels and cover you with dirt and that would be it.

"Macabre."

Then as I thought about the current sufferings of my friends and family, things that I so often pray about, I told Kim that I wanted to see a miracle. To see light break through the darkness. I felt as if God is breaking my heart because He won't intercede in extraordinary ways to bring happiness and joy and comfort to those that I know are hurting.

Silence.

I got home and laid down, unable to sleep because the drugs are so potent, and my head is swimming. I'm tired but I can't sleep.

Suddenly, Kim enters the room and tells me that I need to stop thinking about or setting expectations for what God should do to prove himself to me. I need to stop looking for foundation shattering sermons, revelations of truth, I need to look to Jesus. She told me that He lived, he died, and was resurrected and that's a fact. A statement whose veracity I've been wrestling with for the greater part of my life. To Kim this is absolute truth, but the proof of this was 2000 years ago and now we rely on testimony, written in scripture and exhibited in believers.

There I lay, feeling ill, wishing for a miracle, not necessarily for me but also for my friends and family for whom I pray. But the noise in my brain is deafening and God is nowhere near.

I remember to breathe. In through the nose deeply. Pause. Out through the mouth slowly. Repeat.

I set my thoughts on Jesus and a picture of the cross and I breathe. I imagine my Creator, imagine His presence filling me as I breathe. And then suddenly, a light does break through. A positive thought. I'm alive. I'm fighting. I'm loved. I'm thankful. I can honestly give testimony to a feeling of peace and comfort penetrating me. It's real. I can't explain it.

Now I know some of you will respond, "Brent these exercises of breathing and positive thinking are just evidence of mind over matter, just our body's way of responding physiologically." That there's no miracle. To you I repeat the last thing Kim said to me before she left the room: "life itself is a miracle."

Hmm.

If we consider the beginning of all that exists, the so-called big bang, we know there was some spark which created a universe. And at some later point in time, regardless of how suddenly or slowly, another spark occurred that spawned life itself. Great miracles come from sparks. And as a believer in a God who not only created but sustains this world, I believe that it was our Creator that caused these sparks. And also the very same God that sparked in me the real sense of peace in the midst of some despair. It is the ruach, the breath of life from God.

Breath. Sparks. Simple, simple things.

Why is this helpful? Because I tend to look for the spectacular. A miracle like that which is described in the bible. Seas parted. Water to wine. Rise and walk. A sudden cure for cancer.

I long for a day when all of my friends and family know the Lord. That we would all experience the comfort and purpose of a life united to Christ. That our conversations can move beyond the repeated patterns of brokenness. To enter the verdant pastures of peace (John 10:9).

Don't get me wrong. I'm not saying that God cannot or does not act in mighty ways. I will continue to pray that He does. It's that I'm afraid that I often miss the miraculous while looking for the spectacular. With so much noise and busyness around us, who can blame us for expecting God to shout above the din to be heard and recognized?

But it was a breath that sparked a universe. And my disciplined, prayerful breathing that allowed me to discern a spark of peace. A peace that gave me hope. A hope that roused me from lonely darkness, to get out of bed, persevere by faith. A faith that led me to gather around the people who love me and whom I love. And to know I have been gifted with great capacity to do so. A gift we all have. Our true purpose.

So, this summer, we can marvel at the flashes of lightning from distant storms. The spectacular. And in our yards, we can lazily watch the intermittent fluorescent glow of fireflies as they float through the thick, humid air. A wonder. But inside us, all the time, are the sparks of life. Silent and unseen. But if we breathe with God, we may just sense them. The ruach blowing on them. And embraced, even faith that begins as small as a mustard seed can become as glorious as a spectacular tree. A true miracle.

# Morning Coffee

## *June 11, 2016*

A typical morning for my wife and me is to have a quiet time on our porch, drinking coffee, listening to the birds singing, waiting for the sun to rise, praying, and reading scripture or devotionals.

This morning, Kim got up before me, made the coffee, and began the ritual. I stayed in bed, waiting for a spark. She came back for me, though, sat down beside me, and told me to come out to the porch and "talk to God."

But I knew this morning I had nothing sincere to say. I sat in my chair and looked across at my wife, with her eyes pressed closed, clearly speaking to our Lord. Instead of beginning with prayer, though, I picked up my Bible. I needed God to speak to me.

I came to Psalm 77. Not by some random opening of the Bible but because it was next in my routine reading. Here's what I read:

*Psalm 77:1-15*

> *[1] I cry out to God; yes, I shout.*
> *Oh, that God would listen to me!*

² *When I was in deep trouble,*

    *I searched for the Lord.*

*All night long I prayed, with hands lifted toward heaven,*

    *but my soul was not comforted.*

³ *I think of God, and I moan,*

    *overwhelmed with longing for his help.*

⁴ *You don't let me sleep.*

    *I am too distressed even to pray!*

⁵ *I think of the good old days,*

    *long since ended,*

⁶ *when my nights were filled with joyful songs.*

    *I search my soul and ponder the difference now.*

⁷ *Has the Lord rejected me forever?*

    *Will he never again be kind to me?*

⁸ *Is his unfailing love gone forever?*

    *Have his promises permanently failed?*

⁹ *Has God forgotten to be gracious?*

    *Has he slammed the door on his compassion?*

¹⁰ *And I said, "This is my fate;*

    *the Most High has turned his hand against me."*

¹¹ *But then I recall all you have done, O Lord;*

    *I remember your wonderful deeds of long ago.*

¹² *They are constantly in my thoughts.*

    *I cannot stop thinking about your mighty works.*

¹³ *O God, your ways are holy.*

    *Is there any god as mighty as you?*

*[14] You are the God of great wonders!*

*You demonstrate your awesome power among the nations.*

*[15] By your strong arm, you redeemed your people, the descendants of Jacob and Joseph.*

What would we do without the Psalms?

I'm often consumed with the "good old days," categorizing memories as either BC (before cancer) or WC (with cancer). When at its worst, my fondest memories are tainted, the happy thoughts they should evoke subdued. I picture images of my past strewn across a beach, and I watch as the rushing tide either takes them away or buries them in the sand, visions of future events rolling in the waves, debris from the current storm to litter the landscape.

What happened to the good old days? All around my home are memories of the good old days. Must I look away in order to find peace?

But instead of being afraid to ask the difficult questions of God, to express my dismay, the questions I feel in my heart that sometimes keep me from praying and from living this day to the fullest are written in verses 7-9. Has God forgotten to be gracious? Have his promises permanently failed?

Once again, I must remember to remember. But not just the past.

The Psalmist didn't know this then, but verse 15 has

been fulfilled in the life, death, and resurrection of Christ. God has redeemed His people. Oh how blessed we are to have this hope. Rather than my memories of the good old days being tainted or slipping away, they are being preserved in frame by the love of Christ as I learn to cherish every moment and see them as a part of who God is growing me to be. Past, present, future, all our lives are snapshots of eternity. This is what we need to remember.

I'll close with this. My daughter, Caroline, joined Kim and me on the porch as we were talking. She said, "I can't pray first thing in the morning because when I wake up, I'm usually just thinking of myself. So, I read the Bible first, and then I'm able to pray for others."

And there it is. Wisdom from my 13-year old. How liberating it is to let go of one's self.

The sun is now up. My kids are all up. Time for me to wake up too.

# Yea Though I Walk...

## *June 17, 2016*

Psalm 23. One of the most recognized verses in scripture. Even if you don't call yourself a believer, I suspect you are familiar. In the King James version, verses 1-4;

> *"The Lord is my shepherd; I shall not want.*
>
> *He maketh me to lie down in green pastures: he leadeth me beside the still waters.*
>
> *He restoreth my soul: he leadeth me in the paths of righteousness for his name's sake.*
>
> *Yea, though I walk through the valley of the shadow of death, I will fear no evil: for thou art with me; thy rod and thy staff they comfort me."*

What do you picture when you hear these verses? Myself, I picture a man walking through a dark and lonely ravine. There is an indistinct and difficult path to follow, and surrounding are all manner of threatening objects and sounds and dark clouds that cast an ominous pall. But it is the turmoil inside the man that is deathly.

Some days there is strength to persevere. Other days there is little to carry on. You lie down. Or collapse. Rest, maybe. From somewhere must come the encouragement to stand up and walk, but you feel alone.

Suddenly, from above, at the top of the cliff, a voice shouts, "Have no fear! God is with you! His rod and his staff comfort you! He's leading you to a place of green pastures and still waters. Your soul will be restored!"

Amazing words. Great promises. And yet somehow, at that moment, empty. Strength is not restored. You lie in the valley, unmoved. Not seeing the person but regarding the dark clouds behind them.

I realize that life isn't always this difficult, but how often do you pass road signs, church marquees or hear spoken scripture verses and are emotionally unmoved? And, gasp, have you ever felt yourself recoil at the name of Jesus? Commercialized and misused. God's words. God's son. Powerless?

If so, you're not alone. I've felt this way many times and still do on particular occasions. On "bad" days, a dear friend may, with loving intention, text me a Bible verse. I read it over and over, hoping to conjure that same feeling that prompted the sender, but I remain unstirred. The message doesn't come to life. Its contents remain merely words.

But imagine, instead of there being a voice shouting from the cliff top, a friend descends into the valley with you, offers a hand, pulls you up, wraps an arm around you, and leads you forward. Along the way, he speaks encouragingly: "Green pastures lie ahead. WE will rest beside a placid lake. Instead of shadows of death, blue skies stretch from horizon to horizon, and our souls will be restored from the warmth of the sun and a supernatural presence that infuses the countryside with peace and comfort."

Alas, I can imagine but not envision such an event.

But here I offer a big word: incarnation. Generally speaking, embodying some quality.

It is fascinating that the Bible says, "In the beginning was the Word" (John 1:1). And what's more, "the Word was with God and the Word was God."

All of creation, the whole of scripture, God's revelation to man, is the Word. But yet, in a book, maybe beside your bed, your favorite chair, or perhaps on a shelf somewhere, still just words on pages. Attributed as holy and somehow alive.

How?

None of this makes any sense and Psalm 23 lacks power without incarnation. The Incarnation. God becoming flesh. The Word becoming flesh. John 1:14, speaking of Christ, "And the Word was made flesh, and dwelt among us, (and we beheld his glory, the glory as of the only begotten of the Father) full of grace and truth."

Why does this matter? How is this useful? Because we, as followers of Christ, are called to embody what we believe. In our actions, to testify to the hope offered in the verses we feel called to share, to love by walking alongside our friends and family in need, to remind them that they are not alone.

To incarnate.

Again, a big word. Abstract.

But when my friend texts me and invites me to breakfast at Waffle House, I can't help but sense a deep love in this simple act, as if behind it is the Word.

Others:

"Hey Brent, how 'bout we go for a bike ride tomorrow?"

"Hey guys, let's get together and pray."

"Hey brother, just thinking of you. How are you doing? Wanna grab lunch this week?"

"Can I come and visit you in the clinic while you're getting chemo?"

"Here's a meal we've made for your family."

Voices of believers. Helping hands in the valley. Reminders of green pastures and still waters awaiting us at the valley's end. Strength and motivation to seek out and reciprocate to those in need. Love and encouragement swirling around and even enticing unbelievers to a life of such richness.

"The Word was made flesh and dwelt among us."

I thank God for my family and friends who continue to

love on my family and me. I pray for strength and opportunities to come alongside each of you, if and when you find yourself in a dark and lonely valley. You've displayed your belief. Proven your faith. Inspired me to persevere.

God bless.

# Legacy

## *July 1, 2016*

Greetings friends and family.

I spent the past weekend at the Monastery of the Holy Spirit, in Conyers, GA. My wife had been urging me to visit for a couple of years now. When she senses my getting anxious and emotional, I think she feels that solitude is what I need, some time to reflect and refresh. I can attest that the monastery is most definitely a place of solitude.

It isn't just a place of alone time, though, as there are certainly times when the monks gather. There are 5 services per day in the church, beginning at 4am. The monastery hosts retreats frequently, where they invite outsiders (Christian and non-Christian) to participate in their quiet, structured lifestyle and small conferences on particular activities that the monks themselves might pursue as part of their monastic lifestyle. This weekend was a "writer's retreat," which was described as a time to explore the relationship between faith and writing.

While I went hoping for some personal time, on paper the schedule was pretty filled. I went not knowing what to expect, and, still, my time there wasn't what I expected.

So, why the title "Legacy"?  The Friday before the retreat, I went for a bike ride with my dear friend, Carlton. I was so happy about to ride because it was the first time that I had been on my bike since before my surgery in April. During our ride, I asked him for a topic to think about and perhaps write about during my weekend retreat. After only a few rotations of his pedals, he replied, "legacy."  This subject was clearly on his mind.

The subject of legacy could go in many directions, but, since my personal journey battling cancer has provided the inspiration for this blog, I had to consider the topic of legacy as it pertained to me with the burden of an immediate threat to my longevity.

Two words came to my mind:  affirmation and contentment.

I confess to have long lived my life with a backwards mentality, picturing myself at the end of a long life and facing the inevitable end, wondering if my children, wife, friends, and God would affirm my life as well lived and having personal contentment that it was. This in turn would guide my decisions in the present. My actions. What I produced. How I influenced people. And with these aspirations, hopefully to be content with how I live. Having satisfied the requirements of affirmation and contentment, I would certainly leave behind some useful legacy.

What do I want my legacy to be? In my heart, I hope that my children learn from me humility, honesty, integrity, patience, love, work ethic, and the like. In times of reflection like this, it is easy to believe that this is exactly what my children will take from me. But with five other people in my home, I fear the daily scorecard grading my success with the above virtues as a father and husband would frequently be non-passing. Like in my anger with my children and pride with my wife. And what about as a brother and a son? As a member of my church body? Am I involved and serving people well and sufficiently? And then I must evaluate my overall performance with my job. The people I work for and with. Do they really get my best effort and use of my time?

If I fear daily non-passing grades, how can I hope for a stamp of approval on the sum of my life? And what's more, if the quest for life-affirmation is difficult through the eyes of man, what then becomes of my legacy if the ultimate judge of my life is a Creator who knows my thoughts and my private behavior? Is the pursuit of the "good life" pointless? It sounds like a recipe for bitterness.

So, what's to be done? How can we realize the elusive goal of both affirmation and contentment? A legacy that isn't hypocritical and impermanent? For me, the answer is in the Gospel. In redemption. The last say on life. The fully tallied scorecard of life stamped "approved" regardless of the performance.

I fear some of you may be bored with this story, post after post about Jesus, but honestly, I didn't really plan to arrive at this conclusion; it just made sense all over again. Christ's obedience to death and his resurrection is the legacy we can freely inherit and the good word that we should pass on to the next generation.

As a man, Christ sought affirmation from God the Father, instead of man. And what's more, because of God's promises, expected it. But he lived his life with absolute humility. It was his continuous obedience to God's will, manifested in his inexhaustible self-giving love, that earned him, and consequently us, the reward of resurrection. Life not only endless but perfected. Totally affirmed.

And contentment? As he agonized in Gethsemene over the unavoidable burden of the cross, Christ submitted to the Father, saying "not my will, but yours, be done." And then He said, "Father, if you are willing, remove this cup from me." And then he was abused, tormented, and ultimately crucified.

Contentment?? The description of Christ's suffering unto death doesn't trigger feelings in me that I would describe as contentment.

I had to stop writing. It seemed I had written myself into a dead end.

As I've said, I spent the weekend at a monastery. I was enjoying it, but as of Saturday night, I wasn't sure what I was getting out of it. Saturday was my only full day, and it started at 3:45 when my phone awoke me for 4am Vigils. Part of this service is a 30-minute meditation period. Not knowing precisely how to spend this time, I simply prayed. I prayed for my pastors and their families, for friends in need, for my family. The time passed surprisingly quickly. The rest of the day did too. Overall, it was a long day, busy at times but not without solitude.

I was in my room at the end of the day when my brain (or heart) froze upon attempting to describe Christ's passion as an example of contentment. For some reason, I just had to get out and go for a walk. I found myself on the balcony of the church, overlooking the expansive sanctuary, lit only by the setting sun in blue and purple hues through the many stained-glass windows lining the arcing stone walls. At the far end of the sanctuary is a raised granite platform, beckoning yet mysteriously guarded. And though I never sought to view closely this most venerate area, from the balcony I could see the flicker of a small flame before a wooden altar, upon which rested a spot-lit, open book. I closed my eyes and rested in the cavernous silence. Rather than pray, I emptied my mind. Over-and-over. Disciplined breathing.

And then a thought penetrated the emptiness. "Did I

even think about my disease today?" I couldn't recall. It certainly hadn't been my focus. I wish a photographer had been present to capture my facial expression. Honestly, I think the picture would have shown surprise. Surprised to have had a selfless day on a weekend seemingly all about me. A day of contentment.

In this quiet moment of meditation, when I somehow pushed all thoughts out of my mind, suddenly comes a believable resolution to the question of Christ's contentment at his time of dying. I think I understand more now who Christ is and what He has done for me. I'm sure He was content, even facing death, because He trusted his Heavenly Father. As it is written in Luke 23:46, "And speaking in a loud voice, Jesus said, 'Father, into your hands I commit my spirit'." Are these the words of defeat or victory?

Had Christ not risen from the dead, then there would be no argument, let alone this post. But He knew, by faith, that God would resurrect him, and thus those were the words of the humbly victorious. Battle-weary, most certainly, but content knowing that he had fulfilled his purpose to affirm the righteousness of all God's people.

So my legacy is pretty simple. It is Christ. Living eternally with affirmation, contentment, and, really, all that is His.

Peace and love.

# Thoughts from a Morning Ride

## *July 4, 2016*

Panting, sweating, recovering, I just finished a short bike ride that about finished me. On the last hill, my heart pounding, legs resisting my will, I looked up and assessed the distance, and told myself to push it. I could make it. Then I looked down and watched as the road slipped under my wheel.

It occurred to me that I could keep my head down and the climb would seem to go faster, but I felt myself gripping hard, noticing every bump, and missing out on the pretty countryside.

When I looked to the top, I just reminded myself that I still had a ways to go.

I thought to myself, "somewhere ahead my eyes can find the happy medium between the horizon and the moment. I can loosen my grip a bit, focus on a steady pace, and perhaps dare to look around."

Know what I mean?

As I was considering all of this well-worn-road imagery, I was startled by a fellow rider on my tail. He said, "when I began to catch you, I figured the head wind must be pretty tough."

If only he knew.

He added, "I'm not looking forward to climbing the other side of that hill."

(Seriously? Apparently this hill presents little challenge to him.)

Roused from the metaphysical segment of my ride, I replied, "this is where I get off."

(My neighborhood was approaching.)

Coming alongside me now, we regarded each other. I'm not sure who he saw, though I assume, perhaps self-disparagingly, not a cyclist. But then with a surging pedal stroke, he left me with "have a great 4th."

"You too...." (...pilgrim).

Have a great fourth everyone. Hugs from the Weatherlys.

# A Few Good Men. Or As Good As It Gets

## *July 20, 2016*

"You can't handle the truth!"

Those that have seen the film *A Few Good Men* know this scene well. Jack Nicholson, as Marine Col Jessup, screaming at Tom Cruise's character, Naval lawyer Lt Kaffee, dressing him down for attempting to hold him accountable for the death of a Marine. Kaffee is the cocky, self-absorbed attorney who prefers the plea-bargain to justice. The accused are unapologetic soldiers, trained to value honor over people, and Jessup is the hardened military lifer responsible for guarding the wall that protects our freedom.  For Jessup, the truth is that the comforts we dearly treasure are provided by means and at costs about which we'd prefer to be naive because to know them would bring upon ourselves an unbearable guilt.

Well then.

As I peer out at my life from the vantage point of my soul, I see the wreckage of a wall of self-sufficiency that disease has caused. And yet I see now that it may very well have saved my life.

**118**

My sweet mother loves to tell me that I'm a good man. I may have only just finished doing the dishes, but I know she means it. She's seen a lot of men, been hurt by them, been loved by them and is as good a judge of goodness as there is, I suspect. But every time she tells me this, I cringe. Goodness might just mean I haven't been tempted past the breaking point. Given different circumstances, I might have believed a lie. Instead, I discovered a deeper truth. My need. For a savior. That's the truth that we really can't handle.

One of the most difficult things about making my life "public" is that it is ever humbling. You know about my disease and you know about my faith. The physical and the spiritual parts of me wrestle in my soul like Jacob and the angel, and I tell you all about it. I tell you about my crumbled wall.

I have heard a variety of responses to these blog posts, all of them positive, though I don't kid myself into thinking there are no negative ones; I just haven't heard those. What has struck me, though, is the frequency that I hear something along the lines of "thank you for being so open." That I would frequently be thanked for being open must imply that it is unusual, perhaps even some form of bravery. Why? Because I'm displaying my weakness? That's true. Because I'm trying to be honest about my struggles? True too. Because I'm describing my fears? Yes. But bravery? No. There's nothing to protect. I've nowhere to hide except in Christ. I wonder if the appreciation suggests a hiding behind a wall of self-sufficiency that continues to be protected. Why are we so afraid to be open?

As the title suggests, Jack was in another movie, *As Good as It Gets*. In it, his character, Melvin Udall, has extreme OCD, but, let's face it, he's a jerk. He develops an unlikely relationship with Carol Connelly, played by Helen Hunt. At the end of the movie, Melvin and Carol are walking down a New York sidewalk, when Melvin begins to avoid a series of lines on the road. Carol stops and watches him, and then says, "I'm sorry. Whatever this is isn't going to work." He tries, with a compliment, to convince her to give him a chance and even attempts an awkward kiss. She stares at him as if to say, "no, this just won't work." But then he says, "I can do better" and truly embraces her. A sincere act of love. The possibility of change.

I refuse to accept that my life or anyone else's is as good as it gets, and I testify that there has only ever been one good man. And though I'm someone who sometimes struggles mightily to enjoy the moment, as I live, I continually see before me unlimited possibilities. So why not be open? Not living behind a wall of fear and pride, not trying to be good, not trying to appear self-sufficient, has set me free. Rather than protect an image of myself, I project an image of Christ. All my good deeds point to him. All of my failures are forgiven in him. All of my relationships are upheld by him. New life is conceived in him. Thus, my future promises to be un-predictable, uncertain, and exhausting but never bor-ing, superficial, or static. And to me, that's truly living.

# Harold and the Purple Crayon

## *July 24, 2016*

In 1955, Crocket Johnson released a book titled *Harold and the Purple Crayon*, and it became a classic. It was followed by a short film in 1959 (you can watch it on YouTube, of course). The story is very simple: a small boy, Harold, wishes to have an adventure. Wanting to take a moonlight walk but not seeing the moon, he draws it with his purple crayon on his wall, starkly white and infinitely long and which magically scrolls as his imagination takes him on a journey away from home, through a forest, across a sea, over a mountain, up-and-above in a balloon, into a big city, and finally back into his room, with the moon in its proper place in the frame of his window.

I thought of little Harold the other morning as I lay in bed. Having recently returned, after a 6-year hiatus to Facebook, I'm reminded of the many voices speaking to us about many things. Well, it's been about 30 blog posts now and, I believe, in all but one my focus has been on God, primarily about my faith as I journey with cancer. I considered this morning if I could think of something different to write about, something creative but not spiritual, perhaps a fictional story. But, like Harold's crayon drawing scenes from his imagination, my mind wandered from people, places, and ideas, none captivating me, or it idled thoughtlessly, like Harold dragging his crayon in a line across the wall until he conjured the next scene.

Then my sort of image struck me: Harold drawing me a single, purple dot on his wall. This is where my imaginary adventure begins. I put my finger to the dot and push through it. Then a finger from the other hand and I begin to open up a hole. With both hands now, I spread the hole wide enough to stick my arms and then my head through to the other side. I pull myself completely into the dark void behind Harold's wall. In absolute blackness I reach out for objects to cling to or to at least guide me as I move. Finding nothing and feeling anxious, I run my hands over my face and chest to be assured that I'm still here. I realize that in this world it's either me and nothing or it's me and one infinite something.

My family and my wife will tell you that to some degree I've always been this way, before cancer and even before I made the decision to follow Christ. That from inside of me comes a longing to talk about realities beyond our current condition. That there is more to life than just the scene and the players. And this is why I write about God; He captivates me. My longing comes from a feeling inside me, where another void exists and in which I have my entire life groped around searching for something real to fill it. To use an argument I learned from C.S. Lewis, why would I feel an emptiness inside me if there weren't something to fill it?

For me, the infinite something is God, and this is how I see the tiny world in which we live. Even if all the universe were to fall away, there would still be God. He is His own canvas, which, unlike Harold's, is infinite in dimension and exhibits all of the richness that He imagines. And thus everything is under his dominion. Our most brilliant works, be it art, written words, great cities or technology, are really just collections of His atoms that we've coalesced into something we think matters. And, yet, they are all destined to disappear with the same inevitability that awaits a sandcastle. If anything can last forever, it isn't our works but our souls.

With the time that I've been given, I seek to find the purpose for which I was created. A bird born in a nest becomes a nest maker. The ant is born to its role in its colony. The trees have no wish to walk or fly. All of creation, aside from us, knows its true purpose, mundane and artless, and yet in it we acknowledge order and find beauty. Are we different? Are we meant to find our purpose apart from our Creator?

I just can't escape Him. Regardless of the adventure, wherever I am and whatever I'm doing, the routines of home-life or work, vacationing on the coast, sitting under an umbrella transfixed by the sound and repetition of waves or somewhere in high altitude, mountains stretching past the limits of sight, and even, no, in particular, around people, I know God is there and I'm meant to glorify Him. I am part of something much bigger and something eternal. All of my friends and family, coworkers, neighbors, and strangers have eternal value. I therefore treasure moments with loved ones beyond the mere comfort or pleasure of the activity in which we are engaged.

So, if you're with me, and you see me wander away in wonder, know that I'm probably thanking God for the moment we're sharing or wishing I could say something about Him so we could. Either way, we're basking in the glow of His Light.

Let me share with you Psalm 139, verses 1-14.

> *¹ O Lord, you have searched me and known me!*
> *² You know when I sit down and when I rise up;*
>    *you discern my thoughts from afar.*
> *³ You search out my path and my lying down*
>    *and are acquainted with all my ways.*
> *⁴ Even before a word is on my tongue,*
>    *behold, O Lord, you know it altogether.*
> *⁵ You hem me in, behind and before,*
>    *and lay your hand upon me.*
> *⁶ Such knowledge is too wonderful for me;*
>    *it is high; I cannot attain it.*
> *⁷ Where shall I go from your Spirit?*

Or where shall I flee from your presence?

⁸ If I ascend to heaven, you are there!

   If I make my bed in Sheol, you are there!

⁹ If I take the wings of the morning

   and dwell in the uttermost parts of the sea,

¹⁰ even there your hand shall lead me,

   and your right hand shall hold me.

¹¹ If I say, "Surely the darkness shall cover me,

   and the light about me be night,"

¹² even the darkness is not dark to you;

   the night is bright as the day,

   for darkness is as light with you.

¹³ For you formed my inward parts;

   you knitted me together in my mother's womb.

¹⁴ I praise you, for I am fearfully and wonderfully made.

   Wonderful are your works;  my soul knows it very well.

# Seesaw

## *August 6, 2016*

I will never forget the day that my original tumor was found. The exact moment when the doctor showed me a picture of what was blocking my colon was a drastic shift in reality, as if someone had suddenly jumped off a seesaw with me on the other end. In one moment my perspective of the world had changed from that of a man of good fortune to one who had drawn the unlucky number. The road ahead, once seemingly smooth and clear, was now uncertain and precarious. Contentedly deceived that I understood God's plan for me, I had no idea how difficult was to be the coming battle.

Over three years into my fight with cancer, my body is certainly broken from disease, surgeries and the side-effects of treatment, but it is has been the hows and whys of human suffering that has caused the many sleepless nights. Unable to find purpose and meaning nor to imagine an afterlife, I tend to cling tightly to this life, and clinging induces fear, anxiety, and even physical agitation.

I am certainly not alone in finding myself fighting to find happiness amidst hardship. My family endures this with me and each member faces his or her own struggle. And I know of many friends and family who seem to be stuck in very difficult situations. And I mean stuck. For a long time. There are moments of hope when it appears that their lives might improve, but something happens that undoes any progress. Or worse.

But if I thought my life drastically shifted upon the news of my diagnosis such that I sat alone on a see-saw, I see now that I had misunderstood my faith as some acceptable balance between belief and unbelief. I deceived myself, believing this was life's goal, content-ment. Once my seeming good fortune, from which a weak belief might be attained effortlessly, suddenly slipped away, my unbelief was exposed and, in those moments of despair, was unable to provide credible answers to those difficult questions. To look upon it now is to see my unbelief as a monument to years of doubt, sculpted and hardened by pragmatism and fear. But monuments, though great reminders, cannot give life, and thus to dwell on my unbelief is to be hopeless. And under its power, feelings of longing may suddenly spring, bringing with it quiet anger and bitterness that occasionally erupt in tears. It can be a simple moment, a heartfelt look at the face of one of my children, that stirs these emotions. Hidden despair. This is the dark truth of my struggle to persevere.

But God has not been quiet. He has revealed himself to me in many ways in His provision along the way. Signs. Coincidences. People, places, things. Looking back, I can see it. It's obvious. Still, hoping that the evidence of God will provide the weight to restore the balance of my life is to continue to put my hope in this world, what I can see, touch, and feel. Read the Old Testament, and I think this might sound familiar. Life on a seesaw. Up, down, and, sadly, sometimes stuck in a bad place.

Every seesaw has a fulcrum, the pivot point. For me, the temptation is to let my experiences be the fulcrum of my life, belief and unbelief the rocking, opposite extremes. But God provided another fulcrum, a real one, the cross. Jesus, the man, lived on this earth just like us. It's a historical fact. He was also crucified, another fact. But in the tomb, three days, the fate of the world teetered on the outcome of the cross event. If he remained, rotting forever, I don't think I'd be here writing. What would be the point? You're enduring the story of my suffering because you know I'm going to finish with hope. All great stories have hope, and they resonate because hope is truth. And the gospel tells us he rose, resurrected, not to restore any balance for which we might be weakly contented, but to conquer, to finish. The stone of his tomb rests forever on the side of his death, and all of us are now lifted up to share in his resurrection. For those who believe, our seesaw lives are fully redeemed and we are free to rest.

Believing this story is the choice I must make daily, because, honestly, deep down, I confuse the desire to praise God for a cure with the need for proof that He exists and loves me. I will probably always struggle with this in some way. But he has given me faith. A hope to cling to. Family, friends, His word, and His Holy Spirit to encourage me along the way. Grace, not to cure me of cancer, but to heal my soul. Amen.

1 Peter: 3-9:

*Blessed be the God and Father of our Lord Jesus Christ! According to his great mercy, he has caused us to be born again to a living hope through the resurrection of Jesus Christ from the dead, to an inheritance that is imperishable, undefiled, and unfading, kept in heaven for you, who by God's power are being guarded through faith for a salvation ready to be revealed in the last time. In this you rejoice, though now for a little while, if necessary, you have been grieved by various trials, so that the tested genuineness of your faith—more precious than gold that perishes though it is tested by fire—may be found to result in praise and glory and honor at the revelation of Jesus Christ. Though you have not seen him, you love him. Though you do not now see him, you believe in him and rejoice with joy that is inexpressible and filled with glory, obtaining the outcome of your faith, the salvation of your souls.*

# Health Update

## *August 9, 2016*

Greetings folks.

On behalf of Kim and my family, we thank you again for all of the support we've been given over the entirety of this journey. And I just want to say thanks to those who've continued to read these blog posts while I've been getting treatment recently. Somehow, the 3-month intervals between CT/PET scans has synchronized with the seasons. Kim noted last night that this is the 4th year in a row where we've either been away on the first day of school or have left during the first week. Of course, this is difficult on the kids and on us. But we made the decision to go to MD Anderson in Houston in 2013, and we've got to continue to do so in hope that we're getting the care I need. There are other options, but this is the path we've chosen.

We leave Wednesday morning at 6am amidst chaos at Delta. If all goes according to schedule, we'll arrive in Houston later that morning and I'll have a CT scan that afternoon.

On Thursday morning, we meet with the HIPEC surgeon. If you've read previous posts, you'll recall that this is the doctor that would like to perform a procedure to fill my abdominal cavity with heated, systemic chemo to kill (hopefully) all microscopic cancer cells and any small spots that are present there (they found small "cancer seeds" during my surgery in April). This doctor will give us the results of the CT scan and his thoughts on moving forward. If the chemo that I've been on has continued to be effective and I have no active cancer in my lymphatic system, he might want us to consider this surgery. The problem is that the surgery has "high morbidity", meaning it will kick my butt, and I'll likely be in the hospital for 3 weeks. But it is critical that I get back on chemo as soon as I'm healed up to keep the lymphatic disease in check. If there are any complications to healing that would delay treatment, this could allow tumors to grow in some lymph nodes that would be life-threatening.

On Friday, we'll meet with our head surgeon and get his thoughts. And then we'll meet with my oncologist. Even if the CT scan looks great, he may have a different opinion on whether HIPEC surgery is a good idea. If the CT scan shows progression of disease, well, then we'll have to look for new therapies, and this might mean clinical trials.

So, suffice to say, we may have very critical decisions awaiting us. It may be surgery, it may be staying the course, or it may be a different treatment not available locally (trial). We'll need wisdom to make and peace with the decision, which won't be easy regardless. For the prayer warriors out there, I'm guessing by now you have an idea of how to pray. I myself am praying for my children, my wife, wisdom for my doctors, and my friends and family who support me. Through all of this, I see God at work, and I pray that this never ceases.

Much love,

Brent

# Health Update

## *August 12, 2016*

We're on a plane home. Feeling a joy. A peace. We're having fun. We're still thankful.

Thank you for your encouraging words. It has been great to have received so many comments, texts, and emails. Thank you.

Here's where we stand. The CT scan on Wednesday showed that, although most of my known disease has remained mostly stable/unchanged since the last scan (April), there are some new areas of growth in my abdominal cavity. It seems that the "seeds of cancer" have begun to sprout. What this means is that HIPEC or any other type of surgery is off the table for now and that the current treatment, though slowing progression, is reaching the end of its efficacy. Not to say that continuing the current regimen won't help (I'll be back on the same drugs this Monday), its just that, in the long run, there's only so long the current drugs will keep cancer from growing.

But there's hope! And I think this is why Kim and I feel light and confident. Recently, there has been progress for my cancer type in the area of immunotherapy.

There isn't overwhelming data from the phase I trial, but researchers have found some drugs that may allow some of the recent immunotherapy approaches, which have been successful in other cancers, to be effective in advanced colorectal cancer patients like me. There is a new phase III trial that is now open, recruiting participants, for which my oncologist thinks I'm a great candidate. The limitation is that there are to be only 360 participants or so worldwide, and there will be many people trying to get involved in this trial. I'm at the top of the list at MD Anderson, but it may be a couple of months before they can begin recruiting and by then the trial might be full.

I won't get into specifics, but we have some contacts in a couple of the four current locations that have already begun the trial. Suffice to say, our hope is to be one of these 360 people to participate.

When you start talking trials, typically this means you've reached the end of standard care. This isn't necessarily true in my case, but the fact is, we are close. For me and others, the hope of immunotherapy is what we've been praying for; we have to stay alive long enough for scientists and the medical community to make a breakthrough for our cancer type. They've now shown positive data, and I don't doubt that within a year or so, they will bring a new drug forward for FDA approval.

If you've read my other posts, you know how I feel: God is at work. Of course. But sometimes it feels like He's calling me along a path that He is paving just under my steps. No trowel, no smoothing of the way; of my family and friends, the footprints of our journey will remain. Many are watching our journey. That's our testimony. But to what end? It's tempting to look way ahead. Honestly, in my life, what hasn't worked out in the long run? So I'll stop my mind from wandering ahead of my feet. I'll hope in the new medical advances, but I'll trust in the One from whom all paths begin and to whom all paths lead. I just keep on walking.

God bless.

# *Season 3*

## *Trials*

*Now that the chemotherapy began losing its efficacy and without high-confidence options for a third-line of treatment, after three-and-a-half years of fighting with standard therapies, we began to seek experimental options. Despite some complications, I was ultimately accepted as a patient on a clinical trial. The uncertainty of this period for me was compounded with the tragic loss of Kim's father. After the heavy soul-searching that I've described to this point, belief took on flesh-and-blood at the sight of my father-in-law on life-support.*

# Desiring Heaven

## *August 29, 2016*

*[Note: featured image removed. It was from my friend Carlton and was of a cereus flower, a species of cactus plant that only blooms once a year and only at night. For it to have been this night was a small, timely wonder.]*

What do you think about when you think of heaven? From a Christian perspective, we know heaven as the place where there is no pain and suffering, only the peace and joy of being fully united to Christ. But where is it? What does it look like? Is it a place somewhere in this universe? Or somewhere else entirely? There are a lot of biblical mysteries, but heaven, as a physical place, is impossible to imagine.

I admit to feeling great tension between life as we know it and a life after death, as if they are wholly separate worlds. The sun provides the light of this world, but what of the next? Do new lights come on? Is heaven what we wishfully imagine and describe in difficult circumstances, in particular when confronted with death?

We've all visited earthly places that we might call heavenly. I think of being overcome by the beauty of creation, being awestruck, forgetting for a moment worldly concerns, even suffering, and feeling a pervasive peace filling me through my senses. Astonishing mountain vistas, magnificent bodies of water, stunning sunrises or sunsets at the limits of sight, creation quiets and humbles us. Our greatest machinations or constructions may inspire, but nothing reminds us of our inconsequence and yet makes us feel as part of something permanent and good like the natural wonders that have existed long before us.

On my bookshelf is a collection of essays titled *Heaven is Under Our Feet*, a project of Don Henley's, who started the Walden Woods Project. The essays focus on conservation, a good thing, but the title is provocative, and I think proclaims a common notion: there is no mystical heaven, rather it is the earth that is sacred. This doesn't ring true to me. I think the Reverend Maclean, in the movie *A River Runs Through It,* says it more accurately when teaching his sons about the origins of the earth as he cradles a sedimentary rock pulled from a river: "Long ago rain fell on mud and became rock. Half a billion years ago. But even before that, beneath the rocks, are the words of God."

Heaven is not under our feet; below us, in the earth's core, remains God's furious power to create and destroy worlds. Heaven must exist in some dimension we cannot comprehend. Perhaps it is all around us. Regardless, I see the world we know as a veneer around the eternal word of God. And likewise, our bodies around our souls. Christ was the word become flesh[1], and in Him we are part of that same eternal word.

Psalm 115 says, "The dead cannot sing praises to the Lord, for they have gone into the silence of the grave. But we can praise the Lord both now and forever!" (verses 17-18).  I'm no theologian, but I imagine, to the writer of the Psalm and the Israelites of that time, the praising of God forever was a gift to the generations of His chosen people. But I think, because of the resurrection of Christ, it is a gift to individual souls, too. Death may very well be the entrance into Heaven, but it is our eternal souls that enter, the consummation of the work of redemption throughout our lives. Paradoxically, we praise now because of and despite of our sufferings, but we will praise unreservedly in glory when we understand fully God's plan[2].

Desiring Heaven, then, brings both peace and the will to persevere. Peace like that of being comforted by a parent when a nightmare startles you awake, alone in the dark, when the Spirit assures us that our Heavenly Father is with us and we are dearly loved in Christ and that, despite the brokenness of this world and our lives, everything will be OK. And though often exhausted and wishing to give up that we might enter eternal rest now, the desire for Heaven spurs us to live life purposefully, even fervently. Crying out to the Lord for strength and mercy, we run the race before us[3], hoping to God to lunge for the tape at the finish line, like the Olympic runner, but not to win gold but to bring glory to Him who sustains us.

But alas, these are mere reflections. My thoughts on a subject infinitely beyond the limit of my comprehension. A framework for understanding composed in absence of the crucible of real trial.

On Friday, August 26, we said goodbye to Gibby, Kim's father, my hero, who fought cancer for over 9 years and remained his jovial self, right up to the point when the doctors sedated him for a week-long battle to beat back his disease once again in order to prolong his life. It was close and hopeful, but in the end, it was too much for him. Body failing him, he was placed on life support. Thankfully, his entire family was able to visit him and say their goodbyes as he lay in his darkened room in the ICU, connected to more tubes and equipment than I could have imagined. I confess that this was one of the most difficult moments of my life. As I stood over him, seeing the man at the edge of death, I was overcome with grief and found myself grasping for sincere words that reflected what I really believed. This was no time for platitudes and no occasion to ponder and articulate. My faith was profoundly challenged. This moment was about testimony, and before me lay a man who epitomized selflessness, constancy, endurance, and joy. More accurately, he embodied the qualities of his soul, a clear work of grace. And so, the words were "Goodbye. For a little while."

**142**

Our hope is that God was calling our Gibby home. I felt an intense desire for Heaven, if only so we can be with him again. And, of course, all of our loved ones, those already passed and all we know that someday will.

But it is here that we must remember that the only reason we have this hope is because Jesus has gone before us to the grave and rose from it. This is the crux of it. If the resurrection isn't true, then Gibby is simply gone. But, as if written on our hearts as in the core of the earth, we believe the ancient words, though they seem absurd to rational minds. That once upon a time a man was born of a virgin mother, lived a mistake-free life, gave of himself continually, feeding, healing, teaching, loving, but was killed in the most shameful way and yet was raised from the dead in a new form, similar in appearance to the man but wholly different, and subsequently ascended into the sky to enter some unknown dimension where he now sits at the right hand of a formless god, omnipresent, omniscient, om-nipotent, eternal.

We believe the words not because of some intellectual certainty but because they have filled an unexplainable and haunting emptiness inside; a sense we call "the peace that surpasses all understanding." At times like these, it certainly does.

So, just as Gibby was only recently praising God in a sanctuary with his voice, he continues praising Him somewhere with Jesus and will sing again in a new body in a new world to come[4], where cancer, nor any other form of suffering, has any reign. Only the almighty, tri-une God, who loves us as sons and daughters[5] and is transforming us into the image of Christ[6].

Yes, I desire this. Now and until that time he calls me home too.

*[1] John 1:14 (ESV): And the Word became flesh and dwelt among us, and we have seen his glory, glory as of the only Son from the Father, full of grace and truth.*

*[2] 1 Corinthians 13:12: For now we see in a mirror dimly, but then face to face. Now I know in part; then I shall know fully, even as I have been fully known.*

*[3] Hebrews 12:1: Therefore, since we are surround-ed by so great a cloud of witnesses, let us also lay aside every weight, and sin which clings so closely, and let us run with endurance the race that is set before us,*

*[4] Isaiah 66:22: "For as the new heavens and the new earth that I make shall remain before me," says the LORD, "so shall your offspring and your name re-main."*

*[5] 2 Corinthians 6:18: "And I will be a father to you, and you shall be sons and daughters to me, says the Lord Almighty."*

[6] *2 Corinthians 3:18: And we all, with unveiled face, beholding the glory of the Lord, are being transformed into the same image from one degree of glory to another. For this comes from the Lord who is the Spirit.*

# Good Grief

## *September 12, 2016*

On Saturday, Sep 10, we said our final goodbyes to Tom "Gibby" Gibson, my Kim's father. The memorial service was held at Tom and Kathy's (Kim's mother) church, the Episcopal Church of the Holy Spirit (ECOHS). It was a beautiful service, and we are deeply thankful to Father Oglesby, Reverend Underwood and the other leaders, assistants, and congregants that celebrated the life of Gibby while reminding us of the hope that we have in Christ.  Kim's brother, Chris, gave an appropriately warm, funny, and heartfelt eulogy that would have made Gibby proud.

There are many things I can write about Tom and particularly what he has meant to me as we both battled cancer. But in the process of the Gibson family preparing for the service, Chris solicited remarks from Kim and their sister, Tracy.  I only had the opportunity to read what Kim wrote, but it was so touching that I wanted to share it.

So here are Kim's memories about her Dad:

*Our greatest memories of Gibby are of course all the beach trips we have taken throughout the years. Caroline remembers Gibby being willing to take the girls to the father/daugther dance at their school when Brent was going through chemotherapy. All three of the girls are thankful for and will remember the trip that Gaga and Gibby took them on for the 12th birthdays. Owen remembers Gibby taking him to the driving range and out on the golf course. I think most of the memories and the gifts that he gave to us weren't monetary in nature. They were gifts of experiences and time spent with him. That is a gift that is invaluable and will never tarnish or fade.*

*What we will miss most about Gibby is just being with him. We will all miss his visits. We will miss playing games with him (Scattegories, Boggle, Hollywood Poker, Bingo to name a few), doing jigsaw puzzles with him, and trying to solve his lateral thinking puzzles. We will miss his sayings like "Hey Gang!" or "I need some huggles!" or "Oh goody!" or even when he answers the phone by saying "Yello!" We will miss watching sports events on TV with him especially the golf tournaments. When he would visit, they would always be playing in the background. We will miss his encouragement and just his genuine way of being interested in what is going on in our lives. We will miss just giving him a call to say hello and seeing what he is up to and telling him about what is going on with us.*

*Gibby has many great characteristics. I think the greatest characteristic that has meant so much to me and my family is just his being present. He not only wanted to physically be there for me and for my family but he wanted to be there emotionally too. When you spent time with him, he was not distracted doing other things. He gave his full attention to you. You could talk to him about anything, and he would listen and give advice when asked.*

*Gibby was also genuine. I think he was definitely WYSIWYG (wizzy wig). What You See Is What You Get. He never put on airs and never made you feel as if you had to be something that you are not. He was just a comfortable person to be around. He genuinely cared about people. He cared not only about my family, but he cared about my friends and what was going on in their lives, too.*

*Gibby was a positive influence. Even during his battle with cancer, he rarely complained. He just kept on truckin' (I think I remember when I was little that he had a tshirt with that saying on it?). He preached being well balanced and to live within your means. He not only preached it, but he lived it. He was an inspiration for Brent and his battle with cancer and still is.*

*Gibby was humble. I think this is most evident in his*

**148**

*career. He was a very good salesperson (so I hear from others, not from himself), but he didn't compromise being a family man by gaining status or a title in his career. He just did what he loved to do while putting has family first. I think, especially in the midst of his battle with cancer, he also learned to humble himself before God. He trusted that God had a plan for him and had peace with whatever that plan was. He was not afraid to die. We are thankful that He allowed Gibby to live 9 years with his disease and still maintain a quality of life where he could spend time with us. God was just ready to have him come home. We all can't wait to see him in heaven!*

During the reception following the Memorial service, Chris played a photo montage of Tom's life. I'm glad that the immediate family was able to watch this video prior to the service, because it is certainly a tear-jerker. What stood out most to me was the simplicity of each photo, some little moment of life captured that demonstrates Tom's comforting, facilitating presence. One of my favorites is one of Tom and Kathy and all of the grandchildren sitting on a wooden platform by the water somewhere during one of the many vacations we've shared together. I know it is hot and humid, clothes are hanging on bodies as from a Dali painting. The kids hold ice cream cones and smile obediently, and the photo must come quickly before their treats melt down their hands. There sit Tom and Kathy among them, so comfortable, relaxed and happy, so clearly treasuring the time with their grandkids.

Other favorites are the goofy pictures of the man, and even potentially embarrassing ones, such as him, and perhaps his own father alongside, sleeping obliviously in his chair. Those around him were having a laugh at his expense, and he would laugh, too, upon seeing the picture and never ask anyone to delete a photo that might not have been very flattering. I swear the man had no pride to swallow.

What struck me most is that, for one, there were so many photos from which to choose for the collection, a testament to his presence. But also, the fact that they ranged essentially up to the time of his death. The moments he treasured most were those with his family. He sought time with family all the way to the end. And in the end, there were thus no regrets for time lost, because there really wasn't any. We have "good grief" knowing that he lived life to the fullest and included us and so many others along the way.  And there are photos to prove it.

Yes, happy tears continue to come.  We know death is inevitable, but we see that fulfillment is intentional. I'm reminded that I must grab my shy, cool, or unwilling kids, my family and friends and smile for the camera. Even those awkward, forced-fun situations for which my friends and I used to joke, "making memories!" And, as Gibby before me, when my time comes, to somehow capture goodbye, because it will confirm that it had been love that had made life meaningful. Take all the photos, string them together, and tell a love story. As Kim put it, each experience is "a gift that is invaluable and will never tarnish or fade."

God bless.

# The Beggar

## *September 21, 2016*

Dear friends and family,

Well, it seems there is movement on the treatment front. As I've said previously, it appears the current regimen is finally reaching the end of its efficacy. We've been looking at options for clinical trials, and one in particular is exciting, the testing of an immunotherapy protocol that showed promising results (this was the first-time researchers had seen a response in my cancer type).

I received word Tuesday that I have an appointment on Sep 26 at Tennessee Oncology in Nashville, affiliated with the Sarah Cannon Cancer Institute, to discuss the clinical trials they offer. The immunotherapy trial will be top of the list, but they'll be screening me for all available trials. Though I'm still waiting for MD Anderson to open recruitment for the immunotherapy trial as my first choice, I must explore other options as a backup. However, I must say that I have a good feeling about this consultation in Nashville, something about the timing that reminded me that God always provides. It's as if I feel the touch of a kind hand upon my shoulder as we've started making travel plans.

Seeking wisdom for the decisions we must soon make, my wife and I prayed together the other night. We often hear and pray about God's good plans for our lives; indeed, we believe this notion. But the road can be treacherous. That God is with us on the treacherous path, that's the reassurance.

As I began to pray, I suddenly had feelings of shame. Here we were, entreating the Lord with the same requests that we've made since April 2013, when I was first diagnosed. But actually, in many ways, the pleas have remained the same for as long as we've been Christians.

I suddenly saw myself as a beggar approaching a king raised upon his throne. Instead of bringing him some gift to honor him, I instead bring the confession of the many ways that I've broken his laws. I picture myself holding a large, awkward bag that I've spent the day filling with the refuse of sinful thoughts, words, and deeds, the frequent "small" objects, and then the cumbersome, bulky weightiness of hardheartedness and unbelief. I lay this burden at the foot of his throne, expectantly seeking that it be taken away.

And then this beggar reaches out his hands and asks that it be filled with provision. "Lord, please heal me. Lord, please help our dear friends in need. Lord, please open the eyes of those who cannot see."

Gladly, willingly, into these hands is placed what is

needed today. This beggar may wish for relief from his burdens, to have a year's worth, a lifetime's worth of provision now, but in God's economy, daily bread is best. Otherwise the beggar need not come before the throne.

The reality is that the king loves this time together. Relieving our burdens, providing for us, pleases him. If it were me on that throne, the beggar would have had to make his own way, but this king has a plan to help us tread the treacherous road. Why? Sitting beside him is his son. The heir to all creation. And yet he is the one who descends from the dais in order to carry away the dishonoring offering I had laid. But before doing so, he hugs me as a brother. In my shame, I feel a beggar, deserving nothing. And yet while true, at the sight of that embrace, the king sees two sons, not one. And what pleases a father more than time with his children and providing for them?

I'm learning more to rely on God's daily provision. Looking back, it has always been there, right when I needed it. Daily. Looking forward, I count on it. Even boldly so. But I must wait patiently, even as urgency shakes me. Trusting that every morning, as the dew settles, God's grace and mercy fills our hearts, minds, and souls to persevere and glorify Him another day. Amen.

# Update from Nashville Trip

## *September 27, 2016*

Dear friends and family,

Here is a brief update from our trip to Tennessee Oncology in Nashville. We went up there to discuss clinical trial options.

We met a new clinical oncologist yesterday, and the good news is that we received better news than we had hoped. The long-and-short is, the trial we were most interested in is a 3-armed trial: Arm 1: control drug (currently approved drug for colorectal), Arm 2: experimental drug 1 (approved in other cancer types), and Arm 3: experimental drug 1 + experimental drug 2 (this is the combination therapy that showed some promise for people with my cancer type). The concern we've had with this trial is that each patient gets randomized to an arm, so I might be put on Arm 1 and get a standard therapy (not the immunotherapy).

However, Sarah Cannon just opened a new trial, a phase 1B that only has 1 arm (so no randomization). It is testing experimental drug 1 + experimental drug 2 + another approved drug (one that I've been on before). So, this trial is like Arm 3++. The doctor up there called this the "sexier" option. The idea is to combine drugs that will aid the immune system in recognizing cancer cells so that they can invade and destroy solid tumors.

I need to decide by Thursday if I'm going to get on one of these trials. Honestly, I don't really think I have any choice. Other standard therapies are not all that exciting, frankly. All my docs have said "get on the trial". I don't see any reason not to pursue the newer phase 1B trial. As my friend Carlton said, it seems an answered prayer for there to be a new trial with no randomization for which I'd be the first patient. Crazy. So, assuming nothing happens to change our minds, I'll be going back to Nashville next week for a physical screening. This will involve tests to determine if there is anything that would disqualify me. Assuming I pass that, I would start treatment every 2 weeks in Nashville.

I may buy a small eco-car!

Life may get even more complicated for me soon

Much love and appreciation to you all. Thanks for your continued support!

Brent

# Screen Time

## *October 4, 2016*

Hey folks.

Well, Kim and I are headed to Nashville so I can get screened for candidacy for the Phase 1B trial I wrote about last time. We just found out last night about these appointments.

I won't get into the details here, but if you've been praying for us, we humbly thank you and ask that you pray that these tests go well so I can begin this new treatment regimen very soon (I'm off chemotherapy at the moment).

To our friends helping us out with kids and pets, you are our heroes.

Peace and blessings,

Brent

# Road Bump

## *October 6, 2016*

First, thank you all for your prayers and support.

Here is an update on our trip to Nashville to be screened for a clinical trial.

All was going well with testing until they found that my creatinine level was elevated, a sign that my kidneys aren't functioning at full capacity, likely due to some blockage. The CT scan confirmed the issue. It seems that the tumor down low is now pushing against or has grown into my ureters. This put everything on hold.

We jumped on a plane last night to come home and met with my local urologist this morning, who agrees that the issue needs to be resolved quickly.

So, I'm scheduled for a procedure at 3pm today to, hopefully, insert stents. If he's not able to insert the stents, well, I'd rather not mention the alternative...

I knew something fishy was going on recently. My back has been hurting, and let's just say that trips to the rest-room have been more difficult. Also, they weighed me yesterday at 184lbs, more than I've ever weighed in my life. I looked at my report from 09/26, and I weighed

176. That's 8lbs of fluid buid-up in about nine days!

If this procedure goes well, they will monitor my cre-atine level. Once it comes back down to normal, I can return to Nashville and get moving on the trial.

Please pray that the doctor can resolve this issue with stents and that my kidneys haven't been damaged.

Many, many humble thanks.

Brent

# Mischief Managed

## *October 7, 2016*

Hey folks,

Well, I'm writing this post from a hospital bed at Athens Regional Medical Center (now Piedmont Athens Regional). The great news is that the doctor was successful in inserting stents into my ureters. It was close. He had a difficult time finding one of them. His words were "we got lucky."  Though dazed from the meds, when I lay in recovery and he came to see me, I gave him a big hug. I really needed to wake up to good news. And I told the operating team that.

They kept me in the hospital because I had hydronephrosis, and he wanted to monitor me to ensure I didn't get dehydrated. Suffice to say, I've been making up for lost time in the restroom...

The good news is that my creatinine level has already begun to drop. I'll be getting out of here soon, then its home to rest, work, and to drink plenty of electrolyte fluids. I'll return to the doctor next Tuesday to check my creatinine level again. Once it gets in the normal range again, I can return to Nashville to finish up the screening process.

The comments, phone calls, and texts have been overwhelming. Thank you so much for your support. It remains a strange thing to make your life public, but once you start, it's kinda hard to stop; I assume that folks who are following each saga want updates!

On to the next saga....

Blessings,

Brent

# All Set (Hopefully)

## *October 16, 2016*

Greetings folks,

Sorry I have not given an update since the installation of the stents. It has been a crazy week, and I honestly just haven't felt compelled to write.

The good news is that my creatinine levels dropped precipitously. I'm not all the way back to normal, but my kidney function is good enough for candidacy for the clinical trial.

Kim and I went back to Nashville on Thursday, and I had the CT-guided biopsy Friday morning. Some people have asked when I will have the results of the pathology; I don't think there is any result I need to see (I already know that it's cancer). I think this is just a requirement of the study for genotyping the tumor. I have no reason to think they're going to discover significant differences from what we've already learned from previous pathology, but the study does exclude particular genotypes and they have to be sure.

As it stands, I'm scheduled to begin treatment on Wednesday, Oct 19 (yes!). Kim and I will travel up on Tuesday and stay a couple of nights. Once we settle into a routine, we hope this will only require a one-night stay, but since we don't know how I'll respond to the treatment, we think it best to stay the night after I receive these new drugs.

I'm glad that it is Sunday. I'm exhausted, and I need to hear the Word preached. I long for fellowship with my brothers and sisters in Christ. I hope to humbly worship God. I need to be nourished from the communion table. I look forward to being sent out once again with purpose.

Blessings,

Brent

# Fight On!

## *November 7, 2016*

Happy Sunday evening friends and family.

I write to you from a hotel room in Nashville. I believe I was remiss in not updating more recently about my status on the clinical trial. The great news is that 2 weeks ago I had my first in-clinic treatment. The treatment went well with little side effects. I followed up with pills to be taken at home for 21 days. This went mostly fine as well, though I did break out with a facial rash, but this can be tolerated.

This past week was to be my 2nd round, and Kim and I drove to Nashville on Tuesday for an 8am appt Wednesday morning. Unfortunately, as we approached the city, I began to have serious abdominal cramping, and within a few hours I found myself in the ER. It's crazy to write this, but I had an obstruction in my small bowel! Fortunately, we chose the hospital affiliated with my treatment center, so I was admitted to the Sarah Cannon Cancer Center. I spent four nights there, waiting for things to clear and my system to settle down and begin working again. The good news is that I don't have a full obstruction. The bad news is that the problem still exists, and we really don't know exactly what the issue is. It could be scar tissue from the surgery back in April or it could be a previously unnoticed tumor. At this point, the best we can do is to manage diet very carefully and hope/pray that it resolves with time.

Though I'm still recovering (I have hardly eaten since Tuesday now), the plan is for me to proceed with treatment tomorrow (Monday). If all goes well, we can then come home to our sweet babies that we miss so much.

I have to say, though, that it is times of difficulty like this that the character of family and friends is truly displayed. My mother jumped on a plane to be with Kim and me. Kim's mother stayed the week with our kids. Kim's brother and sister-in-law, Chris and Missy, came up on Friday, followed by her sister, Tracy, on Saturday. Besides all the tasks that came with the job, what touched me most, in many ways, is that they took our kids to our church this morning. I find it funny, though, that none of the kids sat with them, making them appear like Sunday visitors.

I cannot even begin to detail all of the help from our local friends who pitched in with rides, meals, and just great friendship. And, of course, all of the texts, emails and calls of support from distant ones.

Admittedly, I'm struggling a bit right now. I fall so easily into the trap of seeing good health as a sign that God loves me. I say this fully knowing that our bodies are meant to hurt, we're all dying, and it is this brokenness that should point us to the eternal Hope. But I so need reminding of this daily, from different voices and in different ways.

Because we were not planning on being here a week, I required some supplies from home. A $60 Saturday care-package delivered the necessary items, but it was the unexpected notes from my children that was provision my soul desperately needed to hear:

Caroline: "I miss you. I can't wait to see you. Daddy please get better"

Owen: "Remember that God is always there. He is with you at the hospital"

Joy: "God has a plan and is watching over you"

Sam: "Never ever feel let down because of stupid cancer...Cancer is like that really dumb bully that bullies you, so don't let it get to you! FIGHT ON!"

Thank you again, each of you, for your thoughts and prayers. If you feel the urge, please pray that we're able to continue treatment tomorrow and that my system continues to return to normal. I don't know how much Ensure I can drink!

# Light of the Lamp

## *November 10, 2016*

Good morning folks.

Thanks for your prayers, kind words, and support since my last post. You guys are definitely helping us to Fight On! Quick update: thank the Lord, we were able to reconvene treatment on Monday (Nov 7). It was another long day due to snags with the drug companies, as there were concerns with how the recent disruptions had affected my potential contribution of data for the study, but all parties came to a good resolution. I've learned already that my oncologist and the clinical team see me as much more than a mere data point!

Eager to get home, we jumped in the car at 4pm (CST) and headed home. I'm thankful I put new tires on Kim's car, because she burned some serious tread on the highway! I called her Mommio Andretti. We got home around 10pm Monday night. It was SO great to hug and kiss the kids and then collapse into our own beds. Now I'm just trying to put back on the weight, being careful about what I eat. No more yogurt-covered raisins for me!

As we settled back into a normal routine, after the family cleared the house this morning, Cooper (dog) and I had a quiet time together. As my personal Bible reading system would have it, I'm currently in Numbers, Proverbs, and Luke. As I read the first chapter of Luke, it was basically repetitive stanzas of a representative from each tribe of Israel bringing their offerings to the tabernacle. In the back of my mind, I was wondering if anything profound might speak to me this morning.

As I was skimming along through the monotony of Numbers, I came to verses 8:1-3 (NLT translation): "The Lord said to Moses, 'Give Aaron the following instructions: When you set up the seven lamps in the lampstand, place them so their light shines forward in front of the lampstand.' So Aaron did this. He set up the seven lamps so they reflected their light forward, just as the Lord had commanded Moses. The entire lampstand, from its base to its decorative blossoms, was made of beaten gold. It was built according to the exact design the Lord had shown Moses."

I stopped there and re-read it a few times, picturing the scene. When people would enter the room, their eyes would be captured by the light first not the golden beauty of the carefully designed lampstand. In the back of my mind, I sensed a deeper message behind this, but I didn't give thought to it at that point.

But then I casually came to Luke 8, again just as the next chapter in my daily reading scheme. Jesus says in Luke 8:16-18: "No one lights a lamp and then covers it with a bowl or hides it under a bed. A lamp is placed on a stand, where its light can be seen by all who enter the house. For all that is secret will eventually be brought into the open, and everything that is concealed will be brought to light and made known to all."

Boom.

Of course, frequent Bible readers will know this as the 'Parable of the Lamp'.

Reading these passages on the same morning: Coincidence? Sign?

Understand, we can't place too much significance on "coincidences" like these but neither should we place none. For me, and now I pass on to you, these passages remind me that I've been given a gift of Faith in Jesus, and, rather than hide it from the world, keeping it private, it should shine forth such that it is literally the first thing people notice about me when they see me, a light inside that is life-giving to others, although they might only initially discern something different.

I'm not suggesting overbearing or unnatural behavior; this is always perceived as insincerity and turns people away. I'm talking about an intentional concern for others we meet in our normal routines where we simply take notice of them, greet them warmly, listen attentively, and offer our service, if needed. Like the decorative lamps, we are humbled by the power of this light within us. Christ, who first humbled himself on the cross so that he might be the light for the world, in His love serves us in a like manner, particularly as we make time with Him in Word and prayer a part of our normal routines.

God bless.

Brent

# Wander No More

## *November 15, 2016*

Greetings folks.

On Sunday night, I went to the theater and watched *Doctor Strange* with my family. Pretty good movie. I always enjoy the first movies of series where the main character is introduced. I especially love it when they must travel far away and learn ancient practices as part of their physical and spiritual growth. *Batman Begins, Last Samurai*, etc., I'm just drawn to the clash of a Western personality with Eastern culture. Po from *Kung Fu Panda* isn't from America but we certainly relate to him as one who takes little seriously, and I think it is this same theme that I enjoyed in that movie too. So, when Doctor Strange travels to Kathmandu seeking healing and winds up in training in the mystical arts to control energy from other dimensions, I was hooked.

Of particular interest to me in *Doctor Strange* is the existence of a library filled with ancient books containing the secrets of the multiverse. Not simply the universe, an insufficient description of the creation we know, but the multiverse, the many universes of which ours is just a part. It is Doctor Strange's discovery and ability to readily consume the knowledge contained in these books that allows him to ascend to Sorcerer Supreme. That and letting go of his ego which prevents him from embodying this knowledge.

But enough about *Doctor Strange*. I bring it up because I had another "boom" moment yesterday morning when reading the Bible. Another ancient text, although this one is real. I wondered why it is that we can be fascinated with the idea that there could be ancient books in secret libraries somewhere in the world containing ultimate wisdom and yet unmoved by one that might very well be sitting on a shelf or in a drawer in our own homes? As a fantasy, the idea has great allure. But in reality, foolishness?

This is what I think about sometimes when I read the Bible. For me, you could take me to Barnes and Noble, lay the Bible on a table and then offer me that ancient text or any book in the self-help aisle, and I'll take the Bible every time. Ancient wisdom. And truth. Not that the books in the self-help aisle aren't of any value, it's just that I'll look to the Bible first before seeking wisdom elsewhere. I contend that it is truly alive in some mystical way.

The crazy thing is that the Bible is the most readily available book in existence, translated into nearly every language and in different styles in order to be best understood. But my observation is that, increasingly, the assertion of its modern relevance is met with suspicion and disbelief. And why? That's a long discussion, one that interests me but not one I can write in a few hundred lines. But suffice to say that it contains the story of God. Sometimes I want to run and hide from Him too. Or think Him out of existence altogether.

For those interested in further reading and my "boom" moment, have a look at Numbers 9:15-23 and Luke 9:28-36 (biblegateway.com is a good source, I read the NLT version).

As you read, consider that God's Presence is in the cloud. Christ has replaced the Tabernacle. God's people need wander no more.

Love and blessings

Brent

# Numbers

## *November 22, 2016*

Hi folks,

We returned from Nashville last night after I received my 3rd treatment yesterday. I have completed the first 28-day cycle and have begun the 2nd.

I have much to be thankful for, so I thought I'd share.

But first, Kim asked me this morning if I had ever explained why the original name of my blog site was "dbw26.wordpress.com". Well, the "dbw26" wasn't indicative of my having the 26th dbw site, rather, the number 26 has been a magic number of sorts the past couple of years. I can't possibly enumerate the number of times I seem to mysteriously notice when the number 26 is visible somewhere. Very silly, really. I think I drive Kim crazy every time I announce "26!", but the kids have enjoyed it. And pastor/friend Jared thinks I'm crazy, though he hasn't denied its seemingly uncommon prevalence. Anyway, 26 became my number.

The numbers that I really wanted to tell you about are those of a pancreatic enzyme called lipase. After my last round of treatment, having returned home from the ill-fated visit to Nashville on 11/01 which included a 4-night stay in the luxurious Sarah Cannon Cancer Center hospital, I was feeling great and wanting to have some incident-free time between treatments. Frustratingly, the day after treatment on 11/07, I received a call from one of the research nurses as Tennessee Oncology telling me that my lipase level was 3 times the normal limit and that I likely had pancreatitis, an uncommon but known side effect of the immunotherapy.

Ugh. Really?

I had no symptoms whatsoever. Surely this had something to do with my not eating and losing weight (by the time I left the hospital I was down about 16 pounds from my normal weight). But the nurse said, "Not likely. Probably the drug."

They were concerned and were wondering if I needed a steroid infusion to treat the issue. They had me get blood drawn every other day at a local lab to monitor the lipase value. The good news is that, despite having just had treatment, the value continuously dropped from that high value down to moderately elevated by the end of last week. They had me get bloodwork again on Friday, explaining that they'd use that value to determine how to proceed when I came in on Monday for treatment. I wasn't aware that I wouldn't receive the immunotherapy if the value hadn't returned to near normal.

When I arrived at the clinic yesterday, it turns out that they hadn't received the results yet. So, I had to wait in a chair for a couple of hours until they got the lipase test result and the standard chemistry from the blood they drew that morning. I got a little nervous.

Well, the great news is that my blood lipase had returned to almost normal. So that's one number for which I'm praising God, because no one at the clinic had a good explanation as to why it was so high and then returned to normal without any steroid treatment or change in the regimen.

So, as of today, we've completed 3 rounds of immunotherapy infusion, and I've begun my second 3-week course of pills. The hard part about starting new therapies, especially experimental ones, is the wait to determine if the drugs are working. In 4 weeks I'll get a CT scan to see if the tumors in my body are responding to treatment and are shrinking. But I did get a bit of good news this morning. I received an automated email telling me that I had the lab results ready for me to view (from blood drawn yesterday). I opened the results to see how things looked. I can tell you that not being able to eat vegetables is affecting my nutrition, so I'm going to need to address this with supplements and juicing.

I didn't expect to see the measurement of the "CEA" cancer marker listed on the page (a measurement of cancer antigen in my blood). I thought maybe the doctor was withholding this information to keep me from stressing. I admit that I felt a pang of anxiety when I saw CEA listed because I've not really wanted to know, honestly. I've been focusing on enjoying life, each day, trying not to worry about what's going on inside of me. But my eyes naturally scanned to the right to see what the value was. I kissed my wife about 10 times when I saw that it was in the "normal" range. Now, keep in mind, I can't get too excited about this, because this is just one measurement of disease, but it certainly is much better than seeing that it had gone UP since I went off chemotherapy a few months ago. So, praise God. Again.

I've seen good numbers this week. And if you've been reading my posts, you might recall that I'm currently reading the Book of Numbers. What's interesting is that God had shown the Israelites many signs and performed miracles for them, but they continued to grumble and disbelieve. I was convicted of this fact as I read this morning. I, too, continue to struggle believing in God's love and good plan for me. But He is gracious, and this is a long journey. I wouldn't have thought the Book of Numbers would be so significant to me. This time around reading it, it is clearly speaking to me now because I need it.

Thank you so much for your prayers. I know in my heart that they are why the pancreatitis resolved such that the blood lipase returned to normal. And I also know, again, in my heart, that your prayers, said in faith, are why I saw the normal CEA value this morning. My mind still wants to cling to science and medicine and seek answers there, but they provide no rest. Knowing that we, as a body, are praying for each other is a soft pillow on which to lay my head.

We'll continue to watch the pancreatic enzymes and hope and pray that they remain normal. And, of course, that the drugs are doing what the doctors hypothesize they will do. It's a long battle.

Have a great Thanksgiving, everyone!

Oh, and if anyone is interested, the CEA value was 2.6.

Peace and love,

Brent

# Imagine

## *November 29, 2016*

Hanging in the Monarch patio restaurant at the Hotel Zaza in Houston is a large, distressed metal plaque with the lyrics of John Lennon's "Imagine." We stayed at this hotel frequently for my visits to MD Anderson, and that gorgeous patio was our favorite place to relax when away from the medical center. I must have gazed at this plaque and read these lyrics a hundred times.

I remember when I was younger that this was one of my favorite songs. I know now that it is because I really didn't understand the lyrics. But the song feels great. Hopeful and compelling. But as I grew older and began to truly listen to the song, as a Christian I realized that Lennon is most likely describing a world where people are united as one without God because there is no God. And if the world ceases battling for a non-existent truth, then there will be peace. Sorry, but I don't believe this. It sounds like an ever-clashing battle of worldviews. Chaos.

So, I regretfully began to avoid the song because of the mixed feelings it generated.

I bring this up because a couple of weeks ago, our pastor, if I recall correctly, encouraged our congregation to not give up imagining their lives could be transformed by the gospel because imagining change is part of the process of change. It struck me because I have been pondering this idea for weeks now. As he said it, I was fidgeting with my wedding ring, a frequent tic of mine. For some reason, I've been thinking about the symbol of the ring a bit recently too. To cap it off, as this week is the start of Advent, a wreath, a ring of evergreen, was hung on the podium for yesterday's service. I wasn't aware of this, but, for Advent, the wreath symbolizes life without end through Christ. So, these seemingly unrelated concepts have been twisting in my head for too long now. Transformation. Imagination. Rings.

Bear with me now. I recall during leadership training an image that Pastor Aldin used to illustrate a theological concept called "Union with Christ." *[In the post, there is an image. Here, I can only describe it. It depicts six rings, like chain links, but instead of being linked together, there are 5 individual rings linked to a central, "Union with Christ" ring. The other rings are: "Right with God (Justification)", "Made more Christ-like (Sanctification)", "Ultimate Perfection (Glorification)", "Children of God (Adoption)", and "Equipped to Carry On (Perseverance)."]* Granted, these succinct definitions fall short of capturing their full meaning. What I like about this image and what I want to point out is that for followers of Christ, there are incredible gifts, where not only are we "right with God", we are His children and are equipped to persevere through the struggles of this life, which in some mysterious way are preparing us for the hereafter. These rings are guaranteed inseparable, untarnishable, and unbreakable. The gifts they describe enable us to imagine our lives beyond our current circumstances. They enable us to love and forgive one another. And ourselves.

Sometimes, as I fiddle with my ring that I can so easily remove, I'm thankful for these that are permanent. But it also makes me think of other rings and the power they hold when they are yet symbols.

We all know of friends or family whose marriages waver for long periods of time and yet survive. In speaking with them, you hear of times of frustration and moments of hope, but you sense the strength of the union, the vows, a vision of what could be if they hold on one more day. Perhaps giving up the rings would be to release their grip on the hope that transformation is possible. Not just for their marriage but for their lives. I imagine partners clinging to the promises of Jesus and persevering, hoping to experience the contentment that was the promise of their wedding day, to see each other again as when they willingly gave their lives to the other and committing to do so even now, when they understand how difficult that really is.

I have also heard of marriages that have been restored by the exchanging of new rings. Sin had shattered the covenantal bond, irreparably dissolving the union, but the power of forgiveness prevails. I imagine spouses first having to grasp the burden of their own sin, which Christ bore on the cross, before they can be willing to bear the sins of another, forgive and make themselves vulnerable again in a renewed marriage. Humility, thankfulness, and spiritual security slowly overcome bitterness, anger, shame, and guilt. The desire for retribution is replaced by the need for redemption, for both the individual and the marriage. Trusting in their permanent identity as children of God, together they can begin again with the vows that establish one flesh and grow to help each other experience the healing power of knowing Christ more deeply, fostering an intimacy of their souls. And so it is possible for the same two people to imagine new vows with new rings creating a new and unbreakable union.

But if I can conceive of the possibility of restoration of marriage because of the need to believe in restoration for myself, there is one story that escapes the limit of my imagination. I have dear friends who years ago delivered a stillborn nearly full-term. What's more, from early on, they knew the child would have Down's Syndrome and so had prepared, as a family, for the changes their new son would bring. To witness the faith of my brother- and sister-in-Christ during the pregnancy was testimony enough in the power of the gospel, but it was their action in burying their fourth child that awestruck me then and now. Husband and wife removed their wedding rings and placed them in the casket to bury with their son. It wasn't an act of closure; the rings were laid for safekeeping until their glorified bodies can embrace in Heaven, and he can return the proof of their bold promise to be reunited, possible only with the firmest of security in their union with Christ. It is difficult for me to imagine faith like this. We know it is a gift from God, and to them He gave lavishly.

I write about these testimonies because the perseverance of these believers provides great encouragement for me when exhausted from the journey. In dark times, when my imagination provides no vision of a miraculous future, when God seems merely an abstract to explain the unknowable, the story of Jesus rising from the dead a fairy-tale, and the Bible a collection of stories written by uninspired men, it can often be the lives of others that helps me to see clearly how God is at work. And I can imagine how lives can improve if we increasingly embrace the gospel. Including my own. The stories of these wedding rings bring to life the diagram of rings representing Union with Christ, and I remember the gifts. Hardship can and will break us physically and mentally, but the gifts bestowed upon us by Christ uphold us spiritually. And we persevere together.

And so I believe that transformation takes imagination. Life takes imagination. Ironically, listening to the song of peace called "Imagine" takes imagination. To imagine no heaven or hell, no countries, no killing, no possessions, no greed or hunger, and even no religion, is to imagine God's kingdom come. A new creation. Redemption complete. A brotherhood of man in union with God in Christ forever. Imagine that.

Blessings all.

Brent

# Sweet Melodies

## *December 13, 2016*

"When their eye rests on the world to come, a miracle is wrought in their speech so that, in accord with the things described, it borrows from the melodies of the other world."

–Geerhardus Vos, speaking of the prophets of the Old Testament

I can't take credit for discovering this gem of a quote. Pastor Don Aldin referenced it the other night when describing the poetry of Hosea 14. A call for Israel to return to the Lord, the 14th chapter of hope and love follows 13 chapters of frequent brutality, hardness, and judgement. We hear echoes of another world and one that is promised to come in God-spoken phrases like, "they shall return and dwell beneath my shadow; they shall flourish like the grain; they shall blossom like the vine; their fame shall be like the wine of Lebanon" (Hosea 14:7, ESV). Though Hosea often uses harsh language in condemnation of Israel's sin, we find in Chapter 14 words that seem to transcend his personal focus on judgment to deliver a message of healing that emanates from the renewing energy of the perfect world in which God resides.

I continue to work through the book of Numbers. Some-times my eyes just run across the lines without hearing anything. Several times, though, I've stopped in amaze-ment, as I've written about in previous posts. With the seeds of Vos's words planted, I heard melodies of the other world in what I read this morning. Numbers 23-24. The background is Balak, king of Moab, trying to convince the diviner Balaam to curse Israel so Balak's army could then engage Israel in battle and conquer them.

Promising only to do as God commands, three times Balaam seeks the Lord's counsel to deliver God's mes-sage to Balak. Balak, of course, wants to hear a curse, but instead Balaam continually affirms that Israel is God's chosen people and that he cannot curse them.

What's interesting is that, in Balaam's first 2 attempts to seek God's counsel, he first performs a divination rite, presumably with the organs of the animals they were sacrificing. In both cases, the message he delivers to Balak is blunt and dry, as if spoken solely in Balaam's personal voice (e.g. "But how can I curse those whom God has not cursed? How can I condemn those whom the Lord has not condemned? I see them (Israelites) from the cliff tops; I watch them from the hills. I see a people who live by themselves, set apart from other nations..." Num 23:8-9, NLT). His second message is more of the same, Balaam speaking in what seems a worldly interpretation of what he sees: "Listen, I received a command to bless; God has blessed, and I cannot reverse it!" (Num 23:20).

But the third message is totally different. Balak takes Balaam to the top of Mount Peor overlooking an Israelite camp in a desert. This time Balaam "did not resort to divination as before. Instead, he turned and looked out toward the wilderness, where he saw the people of Israel camped, tribe by tribe. Then the Spirit of God came upon him" (Num 24:1-2).

The message he delivers is in a voice wholly different, as if spoken by God himself: "How beautiful are your tents, O Jacob; how lovely are your homes, O Israel! They spread before me like palm groves, like gardens by the riverside. The are like tall trees planted by the Lord, like cedars beside the waters" (Num 24:5-7).

Honestly, the Israelite camp was probably quite a mess. I'm picturing something along the lines of the Woodstock festival. A horde of people spread out in a wasteland, a desert, a wilderness. Beautiful?

As I look out at the world around me, consider the various struggles and difficulties of my friends and family, see the messiness, I try to speak and write words of encouragement that sound convincing and I hope are true, but in my mind, I still picture the lot of us camped in the wilderness, now and in the foreseeable future. It ain't pretty.

These passages remind me that I must remember to

see God's kingdom in its true beauty, adorned with the love of Christ. Chosen and unforsaken. Destined for glory. We are pilgrims in the wilderness, yes, but, when seen with the eyes of God, we are trees planted by the riverside, flourishing together. And as we strive and persevere, the sound we might hear is that of the rushing of leaves blowing in the wind instead of the discord of brokenness.

I can write these words because I hope in the other world. That we're not stranded here but are being led there. In so many ways, we sense it and follow. Balaam knew this, too. He says in his final message, "I see him, but not here and now. I perceive him, but far in the distant future. A star will rise from Jacob; a scepter will emerge from Israel" (Num 24: 17).

That star has already risen. We wait patiently for His return. And keep our ears tuned for the sweet melodies of God's work of redemption.

Blessings all.

# Good News with Heavy Heart

## *December 21, 2016*

Greetings folks

I want to thank you all for your prayers, good wishes, and loving service to my family and me. Kim and I have good news to report. I had a CT scan on Monday, and the treatment I've been receiving has been working. At this point, the only cancer that is visible on the CT scans (resolution > 5mm) is the primary tumor down in the lower plumbing (so to speak). And even that tumor shrunk a little. We seem to have gotten an early Christmas present.

OK, so this is great news. But I report it with a heavy heart, having heard about a couple of tragedies recently, which has made me less inclined to bring up the promising results from the clinical trial in which I'm participating in Nashville, TN.

I'm not at liberty to speak about these tragedies, but suffice to say they involve deaths to young people. And for some reason, its happening before Christmas seems to make it even sadder, though it doesn't change the impact of the tragedy at all. We all know it will make

Christmas difficult for these families for years to come.

When I first heard the news about the most recent tragedy (a deadly car accident), I couldn't help feeling some numbness. Pity yes, but without a hopeful way to explain tragic events, it feels like our lives are often marked by the repeated acceptance of bad news and then a heads-down pressing-on. Like a migrating herd.

But this is no way to live. Numbness is godlessness, godlessness is hopelessness and hopelessness is deathly. We are called to rejoice with those who rejoice, and weep with those who weep (Rom 12:15), not live numbed.

When I received the good news on Monday, I was hesitant to call it great news because that would be cause for celebration, and how can we celebrate while our friends and family are hurting? How can I celebrate when I know there is another test in the future, another result, which, if of the bad variety, might spoil the memories of the celebration?

I can't lie and tell you that Christmas would have been just as merry had I heard that the drugs weren't working. Had cancer continued to grow or even spread, I'd be dealing with anxiety and fear; the great news we received will "make our hearts light" as we spend time with family and friends. But this reveals the spiritual battle, doesn't it? Is my happiness, hope and thankfulness dependent upon bi-weekly or bi-monthly test results?

Alas, my focus must remain on being thankful for the life that I have today. It probably isn't what I would have chosen, but I can promise you that feeling it in constant threat makes it all the more rich because I'm constantly having to remind myself what I find most important and making this my home. I can't help but think that this is more than my own personal condition, because tragedies remind us all that time is short and life is precious.

I may have become wary of celebrating news regarding my disease, but I appreciate the excited responses that I've received from friends and family this week regarding the scans. Even with a heavy heart for those that are hurting and the fear of the possibility that I might have to let you all down with bad news in the future, I again choose to let go of these things that I cannot control in order to celebrate time with friends and family, to cherish being loved and loving others.

And, yes, celebrating the Great News of an event that took place two thousand years ago that no bad news yet has convinced the world isn't true.

God bless.

# Mustard

## *January 11, 2017*

Happy new year, all.

It has been an interesting couple of weeks. In my last post, I reported the great news that the latest CT scan showed that my disease was responding to the experimental treatment that I'm undergoing at Tennessee Oncology up in Nashville. It certainly is nice to report good news. Well, what I've not wanted to share has been the side effects that I've been dealing with. Far be it for me to complain when I want to focus on being thankful that the drugs are working!

To be honest, though, I also want to shy away from saying much about any difficulties for fear that it might undermine the openness to believe, for those reading this blog, that God is at work in my very public battle against cancer and faith journey. I confess that I fear deceiving myself too. But that I have the audacity to believe I can act as purveyor of God's will and purposes certainly reveals my pride and desire for control.

This was made all the more evident Sunday morning when our pastor posed the question: "my life would be better in 2017 if _____". To this question I had 2 answers, one from the head, the other from the heart. The head knows the "Christian" answer, that I would trust God with my life and live by faith. But the heart wants what the heart wants and mine wants to be free of the burden of this disease, of all the difficulty it is causing me and my family. There's nothing wrong with wanting to be cancer-free, of course, but if this desire defines my happiness, then the disease has control over me. Thus enslaved, I'll never experience true joy. A recent warning sign: I apparently haven't been a whole lot of fun to be around lately. So, all the while knowing that true freedom lies in embracing what I espouse, even as Christ beckons, I waver at the narrow gate, afraid the pasture is an illusion (Mat 7:13). The brokenness of my body is a constant reminder that this life is slipping away, and I cling tightly to it, even though I only feel free when I let go.

So here they are, the most recent side effects: elevated liver enzymes indicative of hepatitis. Swollen legs, aching joints, rash, conjunctivitis, blurring of vision. The doctors and nurses are working with me to help alleviate the issues while maintaining drug efficacy. Right now, I'm walking around like an old man.

But it has been the elevated liver enzymes that have been of greatest concern the past few weeks. Though not terribly high, the values have been increasing to the point that I might potentially miss a treatment until the issue resolves. Even after a week of being on steroids, the enzymes were elevated when measured last week, and I needed to get blood work performed on Monday to check again  apparently immune-stimulated hepatitis can get out of hand quickly. I've been waiting for the results.

This morning I woke up a bit early and even rose before Kim. I made our coffee, built a fire, and then sat on the hearth and prayed. While praying, I realized it had been some time since I thanked the Lord for all the people praying for us. So that was my prayer, to say thank you to all the people who love on us in thought, word, and deed.

When finished, I moved to my chair and wondered to myself if my buddy Todd might be interested in breakfast at Waffle House, so I reached for my cell phone, only to receive a text at that very moment from Todd inviting me to "Casa de Waffle". I immediately jumped in the shower to meet him.

Some of you may know Ms V from the Waffle House on 441 in Oconee County. She is a sweet waitress there, and she always writes a scripture reference on the back of your ticket. She gives you the book and verse; it's up to you to look it up. This morning, as Todd and I were finishing breakfast, Ms V, though she wasn't our waitress, walked up to our table, paused a moment as she stared off into the distance, and then said, "Matthew 17:20". I grabbed my phone, opened BibleGateway and read, "You don't have enough faith," Jesus told them.

"I tell you the truth, if you had faith even as small as a mustard seed, you could say to this mountain, 'Move from here to there,' and it would move. Nothing would be impossible." (NLT translation).

Let's be clear here. I don't believe Jesus is suggesting that his disciples, or us for that matter, need to somehow drum up more faith to earn God's favor, let alone perform miracles, but rather we need to live by the faith given us so that we might experience the work of redemption that God is performing. We are both witnesses and participants. So, it was a timely reminder that I need to continue to step out in faith fearlessly in a world of good news and bad. And that includes writing these blog posts. Kim reminds me that our friends and family want updates because they care. Some use the information in order pray specifically. I struggle with being a burden, or worse, a bore and sometimes want to stop altogether.

Frequently, at lunch, I'll bring my Surface Pro with me to do some work or other task, but today I really had no need for it. I brought it anyway, thinking I'd find some use as I ate. On my drive over, I received a phone call from the research nurse at Tennessee Oncology, who informed me that my liver enzymes were perfectly fine, right in the middle of the normal range. So just like that, one day my enzymes were 3 times the normal level and 5 days later they're normal. Once again, as with the pancreatitis several weeks ago, the nurse was somewhat surprised, too; I told her that I had a lot of people praying for me.

I immediately called Kim, and when I told her the good news, she laughed. "There are some crazy things going on inside your body," she said. But I thought to myself, "particularly my heart."

Trust, trust, trust. I don't know God's plans, but He promises that they're good, regardless of how it appears at any given moment. Faith like a mustard seed or mature tree, I owe my life to Him and my purpose is to glorify Him and enjoy Him forever*.

Thankful to have my tablet, I spent lunch eating sushi and writing this post. Ultimately, it seems the purposes of things, small and large, are revealed. I now wonder if Ms V was looking at a bottle of mustard when she gave us that verse.

I can't say it enough:  thank you to all who have loved on me and my family. Though I often feel it, to say I'm in debt would be to dishonor your service. I'm eternally humbled and grateful. God bless.

* Question 1 of the Westminster Shorter Catechism: What is the chief end of man? Man's chief end is to glorify God, and to enjoy him forever.

# *Season 4*

*Living with Cancer*

*Thanks to the blessing of great science and medicine, and I think the hand of God for timing, I began a period of coasting (Kim's word) on effective treatment. For me, I never found a BC-like (Before Cancer) peace, but our family began to relax and settle into a rhythm, despite the interruptions of bi-weekly trips to Nashville. As I continue to stay in the moment all-the-while looking back and asking the "what might have been?" questions, we began to look to the future, too. I think it is this period where much of the great fear left me, replaced by the simple sweetness of moments. And I think I finally came to grips with what I hoped to do with the blog posts, that is to tell the story of God's work in me and my belief in how He is working in the world, despite the evidence to the contrary. I find that sentence funny, though, as reading through these posts for proofing tells no other consistent story than that of the Gospel!*

# Two Stories

## *January 31, 2017*

*[A portion of this post was used in this book's prologue, as it is also used on the "About" page of my blog site. I have left the post in tact despite the duplicated text in the middle.]*

You might have noticed that the URL of my blog is now twostories.blog. Well, even though there is some meaning behind the "dbw26", I decided to change names. For a while now, WordPress has been offering me a real domain name (i.e. not a "wordpress.com" address), but I took some time to settle on what the name would be. Those of you with websites know that it is difficult to come up with a meaningful but unique name on the ".com" domain. Recently, WordPress worked out a deal to create a ".blog" domain, thus creating new space for web addresses. I have settled on twostories. blog. The contents of this post will soon makeup my About page.

So why "twostories"? For two reasons, really. First, because, as you've probably gleaned from my posts, I'm using this site to provide updates about my family's battle with my cancer, but I'm also using it to talk about my faith journey as a follower of Christ. Some posts are both or more one than the other. If I feel it appropriate, I'll put a disclaimer at the top if the post has nothing to do with my health so as not to manipulate those that are reading only for health updates, though it is my hope that you'd read on anyway.

The other reason I've chosen "twostories" (and the site's namesake) is a sermon by a great theologian and author, Frederick Buechner (pronounced "BEEK-ner"). If you want to know what I'm about or, at least, what I hope to be about and think the whole world should be about, then I encourage you to read his sermon "The Two Stories." I give thanks to my dear friend, Pastor Jared Bryant, who gave me a book of Buechner sermons not long after I started sharing online. Being open and vulnerable about your health and your faith is no easy thing, and there have been many times that I have wanted to quit writing due to feelings of embarrassment, insecurity, and fear of judgement. Sensing this, Jared pointed me to Mr Buechner's writing because he thought it would resonate with me, and this sermon in particular, because it would encourage me. It certainly did.

Buechner says,

> *"...to tell the story of who we really are and of the battle between light and dark, between belief and unbelief, between sin and grace that is waged within us all costs plenty and may not gain us anything, we're afraid, but an uneasy silence and a fishy*

*stare." Indeed. But he also says, "each of us has a*
*tale to tell if we would only tell it."*

So, I try to tell my story despite frequent reservations. I'll leave it to you to read the sermon to understand its profound effect on me. You can read it on his website.[1]

I'll end with one short story. My son, Owen, was named after the main character of the novel *A Prayer for Owen Meany*, by John Irving. I first read the book in my early 20s (around 26 years ago). Irving was my favorite author at that time, and this book became my favorite of favorites, though the paperback is long gone. Looking back, I really don't remember what resonated with me about Owen then (that's another discussion), but it was significant enough that my wife, Kim, suggested we give our son that name. Out of the blue, this past Christmas she gave me a hardback volume of *Owen Meany* to go on my bookshelf with the rest of my Irving novels. It remained there several months because I didn't begin reading it again until after my surgery last year. It wasn't too long before Jared gave me the book of Buechner sermons.

The book opens with three epigraphs, one from the Apostle Paul, another from Leon Bloy (French novelist), and one from none other than Frederick Buechner, who happened to be the school minister of the Philips Exeter Academy, the grade school alma mater of John Irving, class of 1961. I find it interesting that my favorite author of my early adulthood was significantly influenced by the man whose writing is having a great impact on me now. Yes, another strange coincidence. Here is the thought-provoking epigraph from *A Prayer for Owen Meany*:

> *"Not the least of my problems is that I can hardly even imagine what kind of an experience a genuine, self-authenticating religious experience would be. Without somehow destroying me in the process, how could God reveal himself in a way that would leave no room for doubt? If there were no room for doubt, there would be no room for me."*

–Frederick Buechner

---

[1] www.frederickbuechner.com/blog/2016/8/20/the-two-stories

# Journey

## *February 4, 2017*

On Saturday the 14th, Kim and I were in Stone Mountain, GA, a suburb of Atlanta and the city where I grew up, to attend the funeral of the father of one of my high school friends. We were spending the Martin Luther King, Jr. holiday weekend together without our children, who were off on a church youth retreat. With no urgency to get home, we decided to drive to Decatur for a late lunch after paying our respects.

We sat in the outdoor area of Leon's Full Service and enjoyed a meal and a beer (Wild Heaven, of course). As we sat and talked, my eyes frequently looked across the street at the four-story building where my father once practiced law from his corner office, about 30 years ago. Having begun at a funeral in my hometown and moved on to a meal on the city square where I many times visited my dad as he worked or met him for lunch, my mind was already drifting off into thoughts of the past, even while trying to give my wife my full attention. Our time there was brief, and we soon headed back to Bishop on Highway 78, past the towns of Tucker, where I went to high school, Stone Mountain, Snellville, where my mother lived after my parents divorced, and on down this familiar road from Decatur to Athens.

Unseasonably warm weather allowed us to put the windows down in our family-oriented Toyota van, and, prior to dozing off to dangerously leave me alone with my thoughts, Kim put on a Journey playlist. "Only the Young", "Faithfully", "Open Arms", "Send Her My Love" and, yes, "Don't Stop Believin'". The songs came alive and brought me back inside Wilma, my first car, a copper-colored (or was it rust? I honestly never knew) Nissan 200SX with a stereo of 600 watts pumping into nearly as many speakers. I pictured myself listening to those same songs as I cruised that same area, but I wondered what thoughts they would have evoked. Plans for the coming weekend. Friends. Spring Break and Summer. College and what I would do when I left home. Not much about school, frankly. Not then. I was having too much fun. Whatever I may have been thinking about as I listened then to those songs, like so many young, I was consumed with the future. I thought I would live forever. With no concern for eternity.

As my mind drifts back, I confess there is a certain longing. Not for who I was but for the freedom. The feeling that now was the moment prior to unlimited possibilities. These days the future feels more uncertain, and I tend to withdraw inwardly, even with company, nostalgia eliciting feelings akin to sadness.

Cruising now, I turn to look at my wife and wonder what future she imagines. She has been at my side or in waiting rooms throughout this near 4-year battle with cancer. But strangely, picturing two slumping soldiers in a trench, life threatened, facing tough odds, we never ask the question "what are we going to do when this war ends?"

In my darker moments, I fear my wife imagining life without the burden of taking care of me. I imagine her life without me. Having known her for almost 30 years, I'm aware of so many of her youthful dreams unfulfilled having chosen a family life with me, not that she professes any regrets. But, if I'm not around, what paths will she take that she had once avoided because they weren't suited for my companionship? And, of course, there would be new companionship. Of course. And I'm content with this. I will always want her to be happy. Just not happier. I have never been a good dancer, while she is one to watch, and suffice to say, chemotherapy hasn't improved my coordination. Will there be a smile I've never seen in the arms of another on some distant dance floor?

When she awakes, we sit in silence and listen to the music. I work up the bravery to ask, "what future do you imagine?" She responds by saying that she, like me, is focused on survival, personal plans not reaching past the following year, making provision for the futures of our children. That means school, sports, work, and vacations. Friends and family. Normal life as best as we can make it.

Here at mid-life, we know we won't live forever, and often it seems we are living in a small window of time that is extended only by doctor's permission, based on the results of clinical examinations like CT scans and bloodwork. We don't talk much about downsizing to the smaller home when the kids are grown, where we could walk together to a market or our favorite restaurant. Instead, we rest in the gift of eternal life, and look forward to the future of futures, after we both depart from this world, however far apart in time that happens. In comparison, all plans are ultimately short term anyway, and we are helping each other live now in that limitless reality.

It may be that there are other arms for her embrace in her future here. There will be other arms for me, too, in Heaven. And the arms of Jesus will provide the comfort to end all suffering and bring the peace we so long for. She has His arms to look forward to as well and knows that mine or any other, though loving and meant to provide these same benefits, just can't; I'm not Jesus. But for the time here, I endeavor to use them working with my family, as we're called, in the dirt[1]. Tilling, planting, cultivating, and watching things grow. Yes, there are and will be weeds, but, as followers of Christ, we place our hope in the promise that somehow all things are working toward our good, and we continue on in faith in anticipation of a great harvest.

So, as someone who believes he is still young on eternity's scale, life still has unlimited possibilities, especially in that place called Heaven. Of course, no one knows what it looks like to pass over, but I picture a great host along the road that leads to the mythical gates. A chorus of hosannas ring out, not just for those approaching, but shared with the One who triumphed and made our entry possible[2]. And if I'm there first and the wife of my youth arrives, I hope to be the one that opens the gate for her, holds the door as she passes through, and meets our Lord. Perhaps I can even make the introductions. And then show her around. That's my plan.

God bless.

> [1] *Genesis 3:17-19 (ESV):* [17] *And to Adam he said, "Because you have listened to the voice of your wife and have eaten of the tree of which I commanded you, 'You shall not eat of it,' cursed is the ground because of you; in pain you shall eat of it all the days of your life;* [18] *thorns and thistles it shall bring forth for you; and you shall eat the plants of the field.* [19]*By the sweat of your face you shall eat bread, till you return to the ground, for out of it you were taken; for you are dust, and to dust you shall return."*

> [2] *Mark 11:9-10 (ESV):* [9]*And those who went before and those who followed were shouting, "Hosanna! Blessed is he who comes in the name of the Lord!* [10]*Blessed is the coming kingdom of our father David! Hosanna in the highest!"*

# Good News to Report

## *February 13, 2017*

Greetings folks,

I'm headed home from Nashville after a long day. We have a pattern with these trips; we drive up on Sunday, have a nice meal somewhere and sleep at a hotel. On Monday, I undergo treatment and whatever tests are required, and we head home afterward. This trip was special because Kim and I took Joy with us (our 16-year old daughter), since she was out of school today.

Today was a busy day. It started at 6:30am at the radiology center for a CT scan, followed by an eye examination. I had planned to get a bit of work done in between appointments and during treatment, but that was rendered impossible because they numbed, dilated and stained my eyes. After the eye exam, it was an echocardiogram, which if you're unaware, is essentially an ultrasound of your heart. Then it was on to the oncology clinic for bloodwork (I think 7 tubes today), a visit with the physician's assistant to discuss test results, and immunotherapy treatment. A lot of fun packed into a single day! And this time I got to experience it alone, as Kim and Joy explored a little of Nashville, and Joy even took a tour of Vanderbilt University. Why not?

It's probably obvious why I get regular CT scans. The images provide updates on tumor response to treatment. The other tests are performed to check if the therapy is having adverse effects on the eyes and heart, and the extensive bloodwork looks for signs that other organs may be affected. The good news is that my eyes and heart appear normal, as does the bloodwork for the things with which they are most interested. In the past, I've had some inflammation of the pancreas and liver, so it's especially comforting to see no elevated enzymes from these organs.

The great news is that the therapy continues to kill cancer cells. The CT scans show no evidence of disease in lymph nodes or other areas, other than the one primary tumor in my nether region (my 3cm nemesis). We saw additional shrinkage of that darn thing too, another 5mm. When we started therapy back in October, it measured about 33mm, and it seems to have shrunk to 25mm, almost 25%. That sounds very exciting, I know. The only question mark was the appearance of what appears to be inflammation in my right lung, so this is something to watch (and pray about), as this could be a side effect of the treatment and could become a problem if it worsens.

We're thrilled that the treatment is working, obviously, but I honestly don't know the significance of the tumor shrinkage. Is my immune system truly attacking the cancer inside me? Is it possible that the tumor could totally die? I just don't know. The oncologist probably won't want to discuss these possibilities yet, either. It's a day-by-day, month-to-month battle. Things could change. But I will tell you that the last time we met with her, she said that she thought they might have found the "magic combination." Doctors don't say things like this if they don't have high confidence. I'm cautious, to be sure, but these past few weeks have been the best that I've felt in a long, long time, physically, mentally, emotionally and spiritually. I feel more at ease. I find myself laughing more often, being silly, and telling even more "dad jokes," marks of the me I remember before cancer began its merciless repression. And for this I'm not only thankful but also hopeful that I'm experiencing some amount of holistic healing.

Thanks to all helping with the kids and dog at home.

Blessings,

Brent

# Tree Hugger

## *February 22, 2017*

Greetings folks,

OK, so it should come as a surprise to no one that I read the Bible with some regularity. I don't follow a set reading plan, though. Rather, when I embark on a full reading of the Bible, I begin at 3 different places (Genesis 1, some place in the middle, in the "wisdom" or "prophets" sections, and Matthew 1). I'll read 2 chapters from each of the OT books and one of the NT as I make my way through. On some mornings, there appears to be no correlation between the different sections, but on others it seems as though I've aligned portions with such symmetry that it speaks to the cohesive, single message of redemption in the unified Bible. The readings of the 3 different sections sometimes seems to unlock some important truth that I need to contemplate and remember.

This morning it was Deuteronomy 19-20, Isaiah 2-3, and John 8. And there was a theme of trees (NLT translation):

> *Deut 20:19-20:* <sup>19</sup> *"When you are attacking a town and the war drags on, you must not cut down the*

*trees with your axes. You may eat the fruit, but do not cut down the trees. Are the trees your enemies, that you should attack them? ²⁰ You may only cut down trees that you know are not valuable for food. Use them to make the equipment you need to attack the enemy town until it falls."*

*Isaiah 2:12-13: ¹² "For the Lord of Heaven's Armies has a day of reckoning. He will punish the proud and mighty and bring down everything that is exalted. ¹³ He will cut down the tall cedars of Lebanon and all the mighty oaks of Bashan."*

*John 8:28-30: ²⁸ "So Jesus said, 'When you have lifted up the Son of Man on the cross, then you will understand that I AM he. I do nothing on my own but say only what the Father taught me. ²⁹ And the one who sent me is with me—he has not deserted me. For I always do what pleases him.' ³⁰ Then many who heard him say these things believed in him."*

As I read these passages, I was reminded to be thankful for God's provision for me and to be wary of my feelings of self-sufficiency. The context of the Deuteronomy passage is God making promises (and commands) for the people of Israel as they were warring with their enemies upon possessing the land that God had promised. It is clear from the passage that God is providing what they needed to live on, food and supplies, and they were to respect that, even in enemy territory. The trees that were good for food shouldn't be cut down, but otherwise, they could be used for means of advancing civilization (I'm extending beyond just the value of trees for war).

The passage in Isaiah was written after Israel had gotten rich and powerful and had begun to turn away from God. They no longer humbly recognized God as the provider of all blessings but began to proudly believe in their own self-sufficiency, even to the point of idolizing things created instead of their Creator. Isaiah uses the imagery of the beautiful, prized "cedars of Lebanon" and the "oaks of Bashan" as symbols of Israel's pride and warns that the Lord will discipline Israel by, among other things, laying low these ornamental (non-fruit-bearing trees). The relationship between Provider and adorer had been perverted; God would humble his people to the point of destroying their man-made possessions of comfort and wealth.

Finally, we see, in the verses from John, Jesus explaining that he will be lifted up on a cross and, further, that something will happen that will make man understand his purpose; that God had sent him to save the world. Jesus was predicting his death but was careful about the timing of it. He was careful about overly provoking those that spoke against him or about publicizing his miracles because his "time had not yet come" (John

7:8). Jesus was to be the fruit of life, though hung on an article of man's war with God, a cross, a man-made tree. At the depth of his humiliation and the height of our pride, Jesus obeyed the will of his father to establish eternal peace between man and God. His ministry and death were the ripening leading to the resurrection event that made the ultimate provision, salvation, available to all God's people.

So, for me, there's warning and encouragement in all of this. I must remember to be thankful for the blessings of this life and humbly live for God's glory, not my own. World history shows that I'm a failure at this, so God relieved me of the responsibility for obtaining righteousness, meaning I'm forgiven because of what Christ did on my behalf. That being said, God did *not* relieve me of the accountability for my actions, because these are the visible signs of the state of my heart, not to mention that detail of their consequences impacting my life and those around me. So, with my heart set on following Jesus another day, I hope to be a tree "planted along a riverbank, with roots that reach deep into the water. Such trees are not bothered by the heat or worried by long months of drought. Their leaves stay green, and they never stop producing fruit" (Jeremiah 17:8).

Peace.

# The Ostrich

## *March 13, 2017*

Many years ago, I was having a conversation with a loved one about life as a Christian. The conversation turned heated, when it shouldn't have. I was immature in my beliefs and was seeking to win an argument instead of being a patient testimony of love. The other said something that has stuck with me all of these years. He commented that the life of a Christian is "putting your head in the sand," because the only way someone could possibly believe in a living God as described in the Bible would be to ignore all of the evidence to the contrary that a rational mind would witness. Christians must naturally create their own reality in order to ignore the obvious, that the world is all that we can touch, hear and see. Stuck in the fairy-tale, we pick and choose those parts of the real world that fit into our paradigm. Head in the sand. Simpletons ignoring reality. The easy life?

I knew it then but I understand it now. Life as a follower of Christ is not the easy life. Sometimes I wish I could put my head in the sand. Or at least run and hide. And I'll tell you why: our lives are not our own. They belong to Christ. Let me tell you why this is so difficult, for me at least.

As I write this, on my left a bag of chemicals is hanging next to me, dripping through a thin tube into a direct line to my heart. On my right is my wife and companion, the one who for nearly three decades has also had a direct line to my heart. They both sustain me in their own ways. Together, Kim and I, along with our four children, are fighting for life as we know it. And we'd love nothing more than to hear these simple, magical words: "you're cured." Unfortunately, medically speaking, there is no cure for metastatic colorectal cancer. At least not yet. And as you're reading this, I'm sure there are some words you'd love to hear. Words that promise peace and rest but which you're afraid you'll never hear.

As believers, we proclaim that all things are possible with God. And so we pray by faith for what seems impossible. And not just for ourselves, particularly for our friends and family with deep needs, difficult circumstances, intense pain and struggle. We watch as the struggles continue, and we resist discouragement and pray again. And again. This is far from easy.

There was once a man, though, who was wanted by the establishment for crimes against the state. He was essentially an outlaw, but he had a band of loyal men following and protecting him. And they went from town to town, serving the poor and needy throughout their country. Fatigue was frequent, but the hero found refreshment in prayer, of all things. At the story's climax, the man and his gang took refuge in a grove of trees, but as they rested, one of his gang betrayed him, selling their whereabouts to the authorities. Sensing his imminent capture but desiring one final, private moment of prayer, the leader asked his men to stand guard as he stepped away to a secluded area. So deep was their exhaustion that his men could not stay awake to do their duty, so one can only imagine how tired was their leader. But here, on his knees, was the turning point of humankind.

"And he said, 'Abba, Father, all things are possible for you. Remove this cup from me. Yet not what I will, but what you will.'"

Of course, those were the words of Christ from the garden of Gethsemane, here from Mark 14:36, willingly submitting his life to God.

Imagine now, for a moment, if he had said, "Abba, Father, all things are possible for you. Remove this cup from me," and that was it. What if Jesus had said, "Lord find another way to redeem your people. Find another way to do your work. I want my life. It is what I value most." Perhaps he and his band of outlaws would have fled. Perhaps there would have been a sword fight and an escape. However it would have played out, it would have been easier than going to the cross. I doubt we would know, though, because it's hard to imagine the Bible still containing a New Testament, for who would have devoted and given their lives to pass on *that* story. Our world would be an unimaginably different place.

I'm not sure what I'd have to write about either. I imagine the cancer would still exist but the hope wouldn't. Perhaps I wouldn't need it anyway. If Jesus hadn't made the choice to submit, then I suspect I'd still be an atheist. I could rest in having performed my ultimate purpose in life, having passed on my DNA to another generation. Are there awards for being a Darwinian Success? A Lifetime Participation award? Not to belittle my life, but really, what good is it if it isn't good for others? If it doesn't fit into a much bigger story?

So, thank God Jesus did make that world-changing choice.

I tell you this because it is the story of my life and anyone else who follows Christ. To submit to God's will is our calling because Christ did so on our behalf. We pray on the one hand for God to perform miracles in our lives and those around us. But so long as the specific thing for which we pray doesn't happen, we are called to devote ourselves to serving others because that is our purpose. If that means battling cancer, then it means battling cancer for God's glory, whatever that looks like. If my part of the story ends today, tomorrow, next year or well after my kids have kids themselves, and though I'd give almost anything to hear those magical words, it is imagining what He might do with me that keeps me writing these blog posts. The inescapable plot of my life.

My hope is that my life is testimony that being a Christian doesn't entail burying your head in the sand, no more than it does for ostriches (that's a myth, too). But if I could go back and have that conversation again, I hope it'd be different. I'm not saying anything dramatic would occur because it isn't up to me to convince anyone of a truth buried deep in their hearts. But I hope it wouldn't be heated. Just warm. Love and sincerity the brick and mortar of lives being built together. One big, giant home where Jesus lives. My life is not my own. And that is precisely why it's worth fighting for.

# Cheer up Charlie

## *March 19, 2017*

Last Friday morning was one of those mornings. I woke up earlier than normal to have some time to myself, and a fire and cup of coffee. But honestly, it was as if I was called to pray and read Scripture. I know this elicits skepticism to some, but how else to explain these moments?  I write what I experience, and here is the log of my morning, Friday March 17, 2017. The players: Moses, Peter, Jesus, God, and, of course, Grandpa Joe, Charlie Bucket, and Willy Wonka.

In case you don't know much about Moses, he was one of the most important people of the Old Testament, if not the. The first five books of the Bible, known as The Pentateuch, are attributed to his authorship. He was a man of God, called to lead God's people, the Israelites, out of slavery in Egypt into the "promised land." I'm almost through the end of his last book, Deuteronomy, and thus at the end of Moses's life.  In the Deuteronomy passage below (32:48-51) we find Moses being called to the top of a mountain overlooking Canaan, the land to which Moses had devoted his life leading God's people but, sadly, was not to be his final resting place. It seems God had held Moses to the highest of standards, and

Moses had failed in a single act of unholiness. While in the desert, starving and thirsty, the Israelites were screaming at Moses for bringing them into the desert to die, suggesting that it would have been better to remain slaves in Egypt. Never failing to provide for His people, God instructed Moses to speak to a rock so it would bring forth water. But, frustrated with the griping people he was faithfully trying to lead, Moses struck it with his staff. Water poured out, but God was not pleased. So God said to Moses, "Because you did not trust me enough to demonstrate my holiness to the people of Israel, you will not lead them into the land I am giving them!" (Numbers 20:12). So, on the threshold of paradise, Moses died. Let's just say it. Harsh.

That same morning, I read John 13. The passage describes the final scene of the Last Supper, when Judas had left the banquet room in order to betray Jesus to the Jewish leaders who sought to capture and kill him. Known for parables and puzzling statements, here Jesus speaks of entering "his glory" and leaving for some place where no one will find him. He then essentially replaces the Jewish law of the OT with a new one, that of love. Understand, I've read this passage hundreds of times and it is still mysterious. Where is Jesus going? Why is Jesus issuing a new commandment? And love of all things. Is this captured in the Ten Commandments? Certainly, love is something the world can agree on (I imagine if someone had a sign in the yard that read "Love one another" there'd be much less skepticism and derision than a depiction of two stone tablets). Then the passage ends with an exchange between Peter and Jesus, where Peter insists that he would follow Jesus wherever he is going, that he's willing to die for him, but Jesus patiently explains that Peter can't come, not yet. And die for him? Jesus predicts that Peter would deny even knowing him. Mysterious, yes. But tender.

Upon reading these verses and pondering them, my mind wandered to the movie *Willy Wonka and the Chocolate Factory*, the original 1971 film based on the book by Roald Dahl. It is one of my fondest, and certainly most memorable, of my childhood. Is it the story? Gene Wilder as Willy Wonka? I pictured the strange contract the children had to sign, with its confusing and ever-shrinking text. I thought of the mistakes, most catastrophic, that each of the children made. Hopefully you've seen the movie and remember. Many scenes are indelible, and I now cannot drink bubble tea without picturing Augustus Gloop stuck in the glass chocolate pipe when I suck a tapioca pearl up the over-sized straw. Well, the "naughty" kids forfeit their chance at the ultimate prize of the movie, a lifetime supply of chocolate. We're not sympathetic, though. They clearly broke the rules, but, more than that, their hearts are spoiled.

As for Charlie, well, there is the episode with the fizzy lifting drink that he and Grandpa Joe consume. They find themselves swimming and rising in the air to their near deaths in a large ceiling fan. But we don't get the feeling they're doing anything very wrong; they aren't trying to take anything, they are merely having fun. And while the other kids are taken away to undo the ill-effects of their mistakes, Charlie and Joe catch up to the group, and we're led to believe they have learned their lesson. After all the other children have been carted off by Oompa Loompas, Charlie remains, and he believes he has won the contest.

But, alas, at the end, it seems no one is victorious. Wonka dismisses Charlie and laments the wasted day. Grandpa Joe is indignant, and he pleads with Wonka that Charlie had done nothing wrong. But Willy, losing his temper, points out the laws that they had broken. Picture the scene. Gene Wilder, hair frenzied, turning on them, shouting, "Wrong, sir! Wrong!....You stole fizzy lifting drinks. You bumped into the ceiling which now has to be washed and sterilized, so you get nothing! You lose! Good day sir!"

One unholy act, seemingly innocent, had disqualified them from their chocolate dream. And there was Moses, overlooking the land he had for so many years imagined making his home, being reminded of his unholy act, one among so many others of good intent, and being told he would die where he stood, banished.

Is Wonka, as Grandpa Joe believes, "an inhuman monster?" Forgive me, but is God?

Even then, when Moses died on that cliff, and, now, two

thousand years after Christ died on that cross, righteousness continues to determine whether we live and die in exile or as citizens of a promised kingdom. And if Moses, a best of men, couldn't earn it, what hope have I?

Which brings me to Peter, the one who first believed Jesus was the Messiah and the rock on which Jesus built his church. But he was also the one whom Christ admonished several times for his humanly blunders. He was the disciple who seemed to know Jesus best, though, which is to say Peter probably needed Him most. Peter so wanted to follow Christ wherever he went, but Jesus knew that Peter wasn't even strong enough to make it through the night without denying he knew him. This never fails to convict.

To the end, Peter never fully understood what Christ had to do. And Grandpa Joe, leading Charlie throughout the movie, stood motionless at the door as Charlie turned from the exit. In his pocket is an Everlasting Gobstopper, a gift from Wonka to each child at the tour's beginning.  Though not unlimited chocolate, to an impoverished boy like Charlie, an everlasting treat would have been a treasure, whether he chose to keep it himself or sell to Wonka's rival, Slugworth. This object, his most valued possession, he gives up. He walks toward Wonka, where he sits at his desk. The half-clock on the wall tick-tocks tension in the silence. Charlie reaches into his pocket, takes the candy, and places the small geometric wonder on the desk. "Mr. Wonka?" There's a pause. Wonka's hand covers the gobstopper, and he mutters, "So shines a good deed in a weary world."* It seems there is a law behind the law that only the heart can obey.

Just like that, Charlie had won. A ride in a magical glass elevator, crashing through the ceiling to hover above the city, the real prize is revealed. Not just chocolate, more than he could have imagined. The whole factory. A home for him and his entire family.

And Jesus? What was the prize he sought? According to the law, he had earned for himself eternal life by living a life without sin, but he voluntarily gave up immortality so that Peter, Moses, and all of God's people might one day be declared righteous and resurrected, regardless of where the bones lie. But to accomplish this, He had to die on a cross. Descend to some hellish state of death and abandonment by God. Rise from the grave in a scarred but perfected form, recognizable only to those to whom he revealed himself. Ascend through the sky into a dimension unknown to man, to rule alongside his Father until their people are gathered. No, Peter couldn't go there, no more than Moses could reach paradise even if he had crossed the Jordan. Because the promised land is more than just property, it is a Kingdom – a Person, a Place, and a People, all bearing God's name. As we find with and in Christ, redemption is one long story.

If *Willy Wonka and the Chocolate Factory* had a sequel, I picture Augustus, Violet, Veruca, Mike, each of their families, the Oompa Loompas, and of course the Buckets, all enjoying a feast together. Because Christ issued a new commandment: love one another. And Charlie embodied it.

In a scene reminiscent of Moses's end, Satan once tempted Christ by bringing him to the top of a mountain to show him all that could be his if he fell down on his knees to worship him. But Christ knew that the world was already his. But what good would it be without his people? We are of much greater value. So He died to bring us home.

–Peace.

* From Shakespeare's *The Merchant of Venice*

*Deuteronomy 32:48-51 (NLT):*

*[48] That very day the Lord spoke to Moses, [49] "Go up this mountain of the Abarim, Mount Nebo, which is in the land of Moab, opposite Jericho, and view the land of Canaan, which I am giving to the people of Israel for a possession. [50] And die on the mountain which you go up, and be gathered to your people, as Aaron your brother died in Mount Hor and was gathered to his people, [51] because you broke faith with me in the midst of the people of Israel at the*

*waters of Meribah-kadesh, in the wilderness of Zin, and because you did not treat me as holy in the midst of the people of Israel. ⁵² For you shall see the land before you, but you shall not go there, into the land that I am giving to the people of Israel."*

*John 13:32-38:*

*³² "... Dear children, I will be with you only a little longer. And as I told the Jewish leaders, you will search for me, but you can't come where I am going. ³³ So now I am giving you a new commandment: Love each other. Just as I have loved you, you should love each other. ³⁵ Your love for one another will prove to the world that you are my disciples."*

*³⁶ Simon Peter asked, "Lord, where are you going?" And Jesus replied, "You can't go with me now, but you will follow me later."*

*³⁷ "But why can't I come now, Lord?" he asked. "I'm ready to die for you."*

*³⁸ Jesus answered, "Die for me? I tell you the truth, Peter—before the rooster crows tomorrow morning, you will deny three times that you even know me.*

# Every Picture Tells a Story

## March 23, 2017

Any dream interpreters out there?

We all know that dreams are like lightning strikes in that 1) you cannot predict them and 2) they obviously don't strike twice. So, when you wake up from a pleasant dream or a troubling one you are either bummed or relieved because you know it won't happen again. But Rod Stewart visited me last night. Twice. Rod. Stewart.

In the first dream, I'm sitting on a weather-worn dock somewhere on the coast with Kim, water lapping against the pilings. I'm putting away fishing tackle because we are about to head home. One of my fishing rods has at least 4 swivels, 10 removable split-shot weights (or "sinkers" like we used to say), and various strength monofilament sections ("leaders"). But I'm pretty sure there is only one hook. We have our Bluetooth speaker playing, and on comes "Forever Young" by Rod Stewart. And I burst out in tears. I'm pinching the weights off, cutting the lines and putting everything back into the tackle box, Kim is talking to me, and I'm crying.

I wake up. (That was strange...shake that off...back to

sleep)

In the next, I found myself standing in front of Rod Stewart himself. This time at a cabin near a lake, similar but different from the place where I spent much of my childhood summers. It's night, and Rod is sitting on a couch, and I'm standing in front of him, telling him what a great voice he has. "Perfect for rock. Great range with just a hint of gravel," holding my hand up as if I've pinched an inch. And then I grab a broomstick and belt out "Do ya think I'm sexy?" while he watches me with a very unaffected expression. When the song ends, I turn to the stereo to change the CD, but I realize that disc 2 of the 4-disc anthology is shattered, upsetting me. (Yes, I own it...I bought it in 1990, ok?)

<<<< Alarm beep...Wake up Maggie, er, Brent >>>>

I'm still unsettled. Of course, I'm now listening to his anthology, trying to discern some hidden meaning.

# Asylum

## *March 27, 2017*

Hello folks. Kim and I are heading home from Nashville after another round of treatment, for which we are very, very thankful. We are fortunate to have access to cutting edge medicine, and, so far, we have seen exciting and promising results. But I feel I should be honest and admit that I'm not always feeling positive and hopeful, even if the mood of my posts gives that impression. Despite circumstances, it is my faith drawing me towards hope. As from the beginning, my darkest days are treatment days. Allow me this indulgence.

It was a typical day in a chilly, fluorescent-lit clinic filled with sick people from all walks of life sitting in vinyl recliners and being tended by like-dressed nurses in purple and blue. As I scan the room to wonder about the other patients around me, who they are, where they're from, what kind of cancer they have, how long have they battled, I know that we all have at least one thing in common: we carry the burden of a percentage, the statistical probability of the likelihood that we are going to be alive in 6 months, a year, 3 years, etc. That's a reality for everyone, but for people with chronic and perhaps terminal diseases, it's a more recurrent thought.

It is very discouraging. You can feel captive.

This feeling is exacerbated by the very medicine keeping you alive. Capillary tubes taped to the skin lead to an infusion pump attached to a shiny metal pole, and you are effectively confined to a chair. I picture a dog tethered to a tree, free to explore a restricted space but frustrated by the unattainable life just outside its reach.

One such dog was our family pet, Eagle, one of several high-end, pure-bred Golden Retrievers that my father kept when I was a kid. Eagle came from a bloodline of circus dogs, so he inherited great athletic ability, as far as dogs go. We kept him in the backyard, which had an 8-foot fence surrounding it. The yard was pretty big, so Eagle had plenty of room, and yet, he still longed for more freedom. Somehow, Eagle kept escaping our yard, presumably by either leaping the fence altogether or by a combination of jumping and scrambling. Regardless, we would frequently wake up and find the dog missing. There were no signs of digging under, so we amazedly assumed he was going over the fence to get out.

In a seemingly innocent and certainly naive attempt to constrain the dog, my father tethered him to a tree inside the backyard at night, so he wouldn't escape. I will never forget waking up one morning, sensing a disturbance outside on our driveway, and walking out through the garage to find a group of people gathered just outside the gate. There, hanging just feet from the ground, hung that beautiful animal, still attached to his chain, which was long enough for him jump over the fence but not enough for him to land.

This image darkly came to mind as I contemplated my impatience, restlessness, and frustration at the need for continual treatment to fight cancer. Sometimes, I too want to do something rash in order to break free, but anything other than contentedly staying the course might be deadly.

Upon telling my wife this story, she looked at me and said with a smile, "That's quite a story! Now why don't you go take a Xanax." We laughed. I asked if I should write about this, and she said no. It's macabre. She's been encouraging me to be more humorous, and this is decidedly not.

Recently, we've been exploring podcasts to help spend the time on these 300-mile journeys to and from Nashville every other week. As we left Nashville today, I put on episode 1 of Lore[1]. It's funny that we would listen to a podcast that explores the dark side of life, given my wife is encouraging me to not dwell on the dark side of my thoughts. Our oldest daughter, Joy, introduced us to this podcast, and we listened to about five of them before we came across episode 6 which is called "Echoes."

"Echoes" is largely about a psychiatric hospital known

as the Danvers Lunatic Asylum (this post's featured image). It has been closed for some time, and though originally a place of good medicine when it opened in 1874, overcrowding and the work of a particularly demented doctor led to the intolerable treatment and deaths of hundreds of patients. Strikingly, at the podcast's end, the writer and narrator makes an assertion about our fear and fascination with psychiatric hospitals that has made them a source of many fictional books and films:

"Perhaps what we really fear is losing control over ourselves. Restraints, locked rooms, medication and irreversible medical procedures represent for many of us the opposite of freedom: the fear of losing our dignity, losing our well-being, losing our very minds. Death, however, is chasing all of us. The curse of mortality is that we are already handing those things over, day by day, until the time when there's nothing left to give."

We gasped and looked at each other for a long moment. These coincidences! "OK, you can write the blog post."

Kim has told me on several occasions that she feels like I'm getting treatment at an insane asylum (forgive the insensitive wording). The clinic is filled with seemingly inanimate bodies. Helpless people, sleeping, quietly talking, others laughing and making the best of things with their companions and those around them. Still, the passive infusion of chemotherapy is not the most human of experiences. It's as if something's being taken from you as you receive it, which I think is what the narrator describes as losing your dignity. It is a reminder that this is not how life is meant to be.

Again, we are extremely thankful for the opportunity to travel to Nashville and for the good news of the cancer's response to the experimental medicines. But, when you are surrounded by others for which the news may not be as hopeful, your mood is subdued. Such brokenness. I so long for that promised time to come when we can celebrate without restraint.

Blessings, all. Thanks.

[1] Lore, by Aaron Mahnke:  http://www.lorepodcast.com/

# Writing on the Metro

## *April 5, 2017*

Greetings folks.

My how time flew. We're heading home today after a week-long Spring Break vacation in Washington DC. Most of this post was written during the time that I spent riding on the Metro train from our hotel in Alexandria, VA to our destination in DC. This has been a fantastic trip, with many stories I could tell, but I have one in particular from Tuesday.

We spent the afternoon in paddle boats in the Tidal Basin enjoying very pleasant weather and the frequent airplanes and helicopters flying overhead, with the Jefferson Memorial, the Washington Monument, the White House, and the famous cherry trees, milky-pink blooms fading to green, surrounding our view. We finished the day with a close-up of the breathtaking Washington Monument, and then headed back to the closest Metro station to return to the hotel. It was about six o'clock.

The Smithsonian station is only one stop from the central hub at L'Enfant station. When we made our way through the turnstiles to get on the train, it was only moments before our first train arrived. We boarded quickly and all but Joy remained standing near the door, since the ride was brief. Soon we were standing on the platform of L'Enfant station, searching for signs to point us to our next train. Joy, though, was frantically rifling through the contents of her bag, head down. When she looked up, her face was ghostly white with desperation, and as we felt the wind of our train's final car pass by, she screamed, "I think I left my purse on the train!"

The grown-ups here, Kim, Gaga (Kim's mother) and I, all had the same response: "it's gone, sweetie, I'm so sorry!" Joy began crying and took off running towards the station attendant's post, not giving up so easily. The attendant was kind and calm, and explained that there was nothing he could do immediately. We would need to wait until the train reached the end of the line, and he could then check if a passenger had turned her purse in or if an employee had found it.

At this point Joy was distraught. She was shaking and crying, makeup streaming down her face, cursing herself and her life. It was here that I remembered who we are. Or at least who we profess to be. Perhaps with no other alternative, I suggested we do what should be natural for Christians in times like these, I told Joy we should pray. My 16-year-old daughter looked at me longingly, the child in her beseeching her father to fix this problem. Then the young adult responded, "that's not going to do any good."

Stunned, but not surprised, I prayed out loud that Joy would find her purse.

It almost sounds silly now to write this. The contents of her purse consisted of a driver's license, a debit card, some retail royalty cards, and maybe $40. All of these things are replaceable, but to Joy these were her personal items and to lose them and have someone else possess them was a tragedy. It was a personal failure.

Kim, Joy, and I took a seat on the dirty tiles of the station floor, like typical dispossessed people, and waited, perhaps half an hour, until the attendant informed us that no one found her purse. It was indeed gone.

So sullenly we boarded the train to head home. On the train, Joy recovered a bit, finding some perspective. She showed us pictures from the day and we shared some laughs.

I've been carrying with me a book called *Well Known* (knownproject.com). It is a series of questions composed by my friends Kaitie and Jared Bryant and is described as "A pocket guide for deeper conversation." I brought it with me to spark conversation as we traveled together, but I frankly still haven't finished the entire book. There are five chapters, and the questions get increasingly intimate the farther along you read. Curiosity overtaking me, I turned to the last page (5.20): "If someone asks you what you believe life is all about, what would you say?"

I read this to Kim and Joy, and without much thought, Joy answered "Jesus." Now, I'm not saying she didn't mean this, but someone who has grown up churched knows all too well that "Jesus" is in some way an appropriate answer to almost every question asked about life, whether or not you believe it. We just laughed, and I pursued no further.

We reached our stop a little after eight o'clock. As we descended the escalator, we realized that Joy no longer had her Metro pass and would thus not be able to leave the station without buying a new card or an act of kindness from the station attendant.

Joy knocked on the glass of the kiosk to get the attention of E. Howard, as the nameplate on the window read. He tried to speak with us via a microphone and speaker, but these were non-functional, so he pushed himself away from his desk, opened the door, and came outside to talk to us. When Joy explained the situation, he asked for her name. Her full name. After she answered, he visibly lightened and pronounced that her purse had been found back at Smithsonian station where our journey had begun. He urged us to leave immediately and to find "Mr. Brown" when we got there.

Though tired and hungry, we re-ascended the escalator to trek back to the starting point of our adventure. We figured that Mr. Brown would be in the kiosk closest to our entrance point, so we bee-lined there and found a genial young man in the booth who excitedly produced a green, vinyl, zippered bag containing Joy's black and white Vera Bradley purse. This time I saw slight tears of joy from my daughter. Mr. Brown explained that only moments after we boarded the first train, someone found her purse by the wall where Joy had only briefly sat before we had hurriedly hopped on the west-bound train. He explained that he used her rail pass to determine our likely destination and had called Mr. Howard to be on the lookout for us.

Joy filled out and signed a required form, took her purse, and we set off homeward again, relieved but exhausted. I began to sing aloud "riding on the Metro-oh-oh," lyrics from the song "Metro" by Berlin. I queued up the song on Spotify, placed a bud in each of our ears, and we leaned against each other as we enjoyed the classic song while the train rocked down the track.

At 9:20 we descended the escalator of our King Street exit. Joy held her purse up triumphantly to show Mr. Howard that it had been recovered. He immediately left his booth to meet us below. And then this large, African-American stranger did something that really surprised me. I don't know what body language Joy had spoken, but he opened his arms and hugged her firmly, very unlike two people that had known each other for only 60 minutes. He told us how happy he was, that he was touched when he heard that a young woman was distraught having lost her purse. He told us that he had prayed for her. This man didn't know anything about us but hated the thought of "good people" being put out by the loss of such an important personal item.

Good people. We encountered several that night. The kind attendant at L'Enfant station who first tried to locate Joy's purse. The unknown person at Smithsonian station who found it and turned it in to Mr. Brown, who made the extra effort to get Joy's bag returned to her that night instead of simply placing it in lost and found, which might have taken days to process. And Mr. Howard at King Street station, who cared, and directed us, and who gave Joy the reassuring hug of both a stranger and a friend in a scary world where you're afraid there are too few good people. So few, in fact, that not even prayer can help.

You can make your own judgment as to whether prayer had anything to do with what unfolded that night. And I'm sure Joy often wonders if this Jesus person really is the answer to questions, like 5.20 of *Well Known*, that don't have easy answers. After she had resigned herself to replacing her license, canceling her cards, and losing the other personal items of value, I admit her answer of "Jesus" rang hollow. But there must be more flesh and blood behind what her response would be now, something to penetrate the heart. I can't answer for her, but there is for me. Had there been a mistake and she had returned to King Street a second time without her purse, I'm certain she still would have found a hug waiting for her. Because the reassurance conveyed by such gestures isn't about happy endings to bad days, it's that there is love and even control outside of the God-world it may sometimes seem we've created for our own comfort and safety but abandon upon the crash of reality. Three hours on a subway train and we found more than a lost purse. Good people and a critical question, circumstance and timely coincide, kindness and, yes, prayer, working together to give us hope, we found just one more reason to believe. Yeah, I think this is what life's all about. I realized it as Joy looked up and said, "thank you."

# Quick Health Post

## *April 10, 2017*

Hey folks

Kim and I are headed to Nashville for bi-monthly treatment tomorrow. I'm also getting a CT Scan in the morning. We appreciate all of your prayers and encouragement and the other myriad expressions of love and support.

Love and blessings,

Brent

# Celebrating Life

## *April 12, 2017*

Hello friends and family,

I just wanted to let y'all know that all is stable on the cancer front. The CT scan report from Monday showed that the size of the primary tumor is unchanged from the scans of 8 weeks ago and that the "nodal infiltrates" that were visible in my lungs had basically resolved, presumably confirming that this was inflammation and nothing to worry about.

I was in the office with Kim when the oncologist came in and gave me the good news that the disease was stable. Kim said the blood drained from my face. At that moment, "stable" meant "no longer being crushed into oblivion, never to return" and so I got spooked. I turned into Casper, by the unfriendly ghost of fear. I have to be reminded that living and thriving are very good things. The oncologist is thrilled that it seems we have found the right balance of drug efficacy and side effect minimization. I must be a patient patient. Thank you, Lord. And thank you to all who have been praying for us. And to my friends and family out there fighting this disease, know that I love you and pray for you.

Yesterday was the birthday of my twin daughters, Caroline and Samantha. It also happens to be the 4-year anniversary of the diagnosis of my cancer. I had that ill-fated colonoscopy on their birthday back in 2013, not expecting that I would forever associate their special day with "the curse".

Right now, the extra significance allows us to celebrate the life we share. But someday it may be that they just want to stay in bed instead of facing a day that reminds them of death (sorry to be so blunt). I got a glimpse of this when I awoke yesterday morning as Caroline came in crying to my bedside. She missed her grandfather, Gibby, who died last year of cancer. And, of course, there is her father, resting from the previous day's trip out of town for treatment for this same indifferent killer. Reminders of the brokenness of this world on a child's birthday. Ugh.

My hope for them as they get older, regardless of who is or isn't around the table when their birthday cakes are cut, is that they remember the preciousness of life and thus celebrate that day with fervor, appreciating every lit candle. And if there are tears, I want them to be tears of joy and not sadness. Remembrance, appreciation, anticipation, and excitement putting appropriate smiles on their faces.

And we saw these smiling faces last night as we celebrated their 14th birthdays. I love these girls so, so much. They are as different in personality as they are in appearance. They have unique gifts (and needs). As Kim reminded me in a recent Instagram post, next year they will attend different high schools, which brings its own uncertainty and excitement. I look forward to April 11, 2018 when we all celebrate these next 12 months together. I can't wait to see what happens next with these beautiful kids and our crazy lives.

Blessings all.

# Voices

## *April 14, 2017*

Greetings folks,

I swear, my intention is not to blow up your inbox with blog posts. I tell myself to take a break, be careful not to be over-exposed. Ha. As if that hasn't already occurred. But unexpectedly, something will happen that my brain won't stop fixating on, and I just have to get it out. I never knew I had so much to say until I started talking. Well, writing, as it were.

Today is 04/14/17, Easter weekend. Thursday night was a nice, relaxing evening. I picked up groceries for dinner. I came home to an open bottle of Rosé. I wrapped prosciutto around asparagus, prepped and began baking red potatoes, and lit the Big Green Egg. Kim and I sat outside enjoying the short-lived, bug-free (and thus deet-free) air, drinking a glass of wine, waiting for the grill to heat. My daughter, Joy, joined us. It was easy.

My wife told me that the day had been a difficult one for her mother, Gaga, though. It was a year ago that I had the failed surgery to remove the tumor down in the "sewer." It was also the day that the health of Kim's father, Gibby, began to decline, starting with a trip to the ER on the same day I had surgery. What a difficult day that was for our family! The resiliency of my children amazes me.

And then, on the day the US dropped "the mother of all bombs" on Afghanistan, Kim dropped one on me: "When you came out of surgery that day, having spoken to the doctor and done some research on the web, I didn't expect that you'd be here today."

Boom.

Well, here I am, cooking salmon on a Thursday night.

The post from Wednesday ("Celebrating Life") came after a rather difficult Tuesday, which came after the typically surreal Monday of treatment and CT scanning in a foreign city. I was really struggling on Tuesday. I was agitated and emotional, burdened. I had the realization that I'm fighting two cancers: on one front, the tumor and microscopic metastatic disease and, on the other, doubt in God and all his goodness. And when additional worldly problems occur, as happened this week, I want to scream. Or at least talk very loudly to Kim. Honestly, I want the two cancers to simply disappear, even though I know that somehow the struggle with both is changing me, growing me, hopefully for the better.

After stunning me (and Joy), my wife entered the house to grab MY bible (she's typically a phone-Bible person). She opened and began reading Hebrews 3, the chapter she had read at 4:30 that morning when she was unable to sleep. Speaking of the forever wandering Israelites, the writer says, "So we see that because of their unbelief they were not able to enter his rest" (Hebrews 3:19, NLT). We can define rest in many ways and there is always a risk of taking scripture out of context and using it for our own purposes, but Kim's message to me was that I'm exhausted from fighting in large part because of my lifelong struggle with unbelief. Though I know I'm cured, in a spiritual sense, the "old man" in me has some serious baggage. So on days like Tuesday I'm unable to find rest.

But there is encouragement for me and for those that empathize. From 3:15, "Remember what it [Psalm 95] says: 'Today when you hear his voice, don't harden your hearts as Israel did when they rebelled.'"

What exactly does that mean?

Here are my thoughts.

We have an expression in the church, for those who are considering and have the opportunity to be ordained to some office, be it deacon, elder, pastor: external call and internal call. The external call is the voice of friends and family who encourage someone to pursue formal service, and the internal call is that voice inside that urges one to do it. The two calls can confirm your purpose, but sometimes there may be confusion. These are varied voices after all. Still, it is critical to listen to both, albeit discerningly.

My pastor/friend/brother, Jared, has frequently told me that, in those times when he is questioning his call to be a pastor (internal), he continues to hear words of support from others that his work is meaningful, helpful, and needed (external). And in the midst of the conflicting voices, he explains that he takes the external call very seriously, because it just may be the voice of God. (OK, he never actually said it like that, but I think this is what it comes down to).

And so, from time to time, I sit at my computer and tell a bit of my story. And when I write, I know what I'm trying to communicate. I have an expectation for how people might respond. And when I say that the tumor is stable but was spooked because it didn't continue to shrink, I'm saying I'm unsure of how to feel. I guess I'm mostly happy that the situation hasn't worsened. It could be good news, but how can we be sure it's not just a snapshot between the transition from great to bad? When I say "Thank you Lord," I'm not raising my hands and shouting PTLs (praise-the-Lords). I'm willfully submitting my appreciation to God out of a hope that He's in control. Choosing to believe. Acting in faith.

Social media is a fickle thing. Sometimes you get crickets. Sometimes you might get vitriol, though I avoid trying to say anything controversial, other than occasionally writing a little about a man named Jesus. And then sometimes there's an outpouring of support and unexpected responses, like "Great News!" and "Praise God!" that I saw with Wednesday's post. Wasn't feeling that. Wasn't expecting that. So many external voices in unison, conflicting with the one, sometimes doubting, voice inside. Could it be? "THE" Voice?

So, we must listen. We must also encourage and speak truth to each other. Kim didn't expect me to be here a year after they discovered inoperable disease in my abdomen. Honestly, maybe I didn't either. But it is safe to say that the "Great news!" that has been proclaimed at critical times over the past several years has indeed been so, because it has always been an encouraging reminder that we're not alone. And I'm still here, dang it!

I'm listening to you. I so appreciate you. Though I struggle and fret, in the comfort of such great love and support I find rest. Thanks again.

Have a great Easter! (PTL)

# Elephant

## *May 6, 2017*

In the movie *Good Morning Vietnam*, the dull and witless Lt. Steven Hauk is replaced as deejay by the irrepressible Robin Williams, playing Adrian Cronauer. When the commanding officer informs Lt Hauk that he'd no longer be working behind the mic, Lt. Hauk responds, "Sir, in my heart I know I'm funny." I think I'm funny, but maybe that only comes out when you're with me. Kim wants me to lighten up and write about something funny. Well, when I told her the following, I was smiling. Does that count?

The other day I was sitting at my desk at work, listening to a playlist of music from Jason Isbell, one of my favorite singer-songwriters. The song "Elephant" came on. In his own words, it's "the saddest song ever." It's about a friend of his who is dying of cancer, and they try to live and enjoy a normal life together while trying to "ignore the elephant in the room." The song is sad. And I skipped it.

I looked it up online, and it appears that the expression "elephant in the room" has been around since the early 1800s to refer to an obvious problem that no one wants to discuss. I've certainly had experience with this feeling, being somewhat familiar with the subject of Isbell's song. But, while I get the point of the "metaphorical idiom" being employed, I don't quite know what to do with an elephant. It probably is best to ignore it. I know that mouse-sized talk won't scare it away. But I think a more accurate metaphor, and one I can better exploit, is to refer to the unheeded object as a coffin. A casket. After all, if you're talking to someone howdah'd (a saddle for elephants) with a deadly disease, the Spectre of Death is really the obvious thing that is often ignored. And to the idea of a "coffin in the room," I say Amen. There are many things I'd like to put to death right now in order to cultivate inside of me that which is imperishable. And imagining myself placing my brokenness into a coffin provides some strange relief. It's liberating. And it's something we all can experience. Together.

Being a friend, a brother, a husband, a father, a member of a church body, there are certainly plenty of opportunities to hear about the difficulties that others are experiencing. And I want nothing more than to listen and offer any help that I might be able to provide, but often, again because of the darn cancer elephant, er coffin, I hear something along the lines of, "but this is nothing compared to what you're going through." I dismiss this, of course, because I consider the difficulties that everyone experiences important. At awkward moments like these, it would be freeing to say, "yes, there's my coffin, it's right there. It's a beautiful, sturdy box of polished wood and is lined inside with fine upholstery. Someday they will lay my body in it, but it will never hold my soul. And what's more, the casket is open, you can look inside, there lies all the fear that too often grips me, but there also is my unbelief, my mistakes of the past, my shame and guilt. There it all is. I have to bear the burden of this brokenness until they put my body in that coffin and lower it into the dirt." And it's then that someone who loves me responds, "I'll help you carry it." This has been my life, exposed but oh so well loved and supported.

You see, to be open, to be vulnerable, to let others know you, is to not only receive help but it is also to encourage others to do the same. Once we've acknowledged my coffin, we can shut the lid, and then we can talk about your problems, your mess, your brokenness. And hopefully we can put that stuff in a coffin of your own. I know it isn't easy. I know my fear and unbelief won't stay dead, and your struggles won't either. So we help each other put to death our sin and brokenness and we help each other bear the pain and scars they create. The coffins are real. And they're heavy. But we carry them until death. Yes, we're pallbearers.

The apostle Paul, in 2 Corinthians 4, says, "[8] We are afflicted in every way, but not crushed; perplexed, but not driven to despair; [9] persecuted, but not forsaken; struck down, but not destroyed; always carrying in the body the death of Jesus, so that the life of Jesus may also be manifested in our bodies."

"...always carrying in the body the death of Jesus..." Like I said, heavy.

But in verse 7 Paul also gives us one of the most well-known expressions from the New Testament, the notion that our bodies are jars of clay. Earthen vessels for the gift of Christ living within us. That's what should be acknowledged but what is really often ignored.

Picture now these broken things, including our bodies, filling a casket. And we know its destination: the ground. Gone. Forever. The stout wooden vessel and the earthen jar, our bones and all, return to dust. But our souls, the imperishable part of us united to God in Christ and preserved in life in jars of clay, carry on, someday to return to re-form our bodies from the dust, leaving behind the broken particles, to resurrect our glorified selves.

And here is where life is beautiful. There is an imperishable light within us that we live for now, and we can actively separate ourselves from the death we bear. We can push brokenness away, into a coffin as it were, and live the most fulfilling of lives apart from it, even while our hands grasp the casket's rails. Around us are those helping to carry it, and perhaps so lightened, we are able to reach out to help others who are weary.

And then there is the time when we can lay the caskets down. We can't bury them yet, but we can rest together. There is sweet ease in knowing one another deeply and simply enjoying sincere company. I think this is what we all desire during family dinners, on date nights, boys' and girls' road trips, reunions, and Sundays. The moments when we set aside the caskets in fellowship. Not ignoring them but experiencing new life without them.

People and coffins together. Can you picture such strange scenes as these? Would they be somber like a funeral? I suspect laughter would break out with the release of tension in finding that we are so connected, just as Adrian Cronauer discovered as he was leaving Vietnam. Bottled-up and frustrated, he was coaxed for one last yawp of "Good Morning Vietnam!" which turned out to be the release he needed, off-air and personal to a caravan of men facing death. Yes, laughter is often the best and most appropriate medicine for difficult circumstances. Joy made possible by acknowledging the coffin in the room. Blessings, all.

# Fields of Dover

## *May 21, 2017*

I really don't know. It's been 6 weeks since the last CT scan, and I don't have any updates on my condition, other than to mention a couple of lab results that showed some elevated measurements that required follow-up diagnostics to monitor possible side-effects from treatment. The protocol for one of these results required that I urinate in a jug for 24 hours.

That day was another which made me thankful for my job, which allows me to work from home on days like that. I realize that I probably should have written something about these tests beforehand to facilitate the support of prayer and "positive vibes," but I didn't feel up to it at the time. Well, the jug thing could be a regular event prior to treatment, so I may yet need them.

As I sat on my porch this morning, listening in the dark to the varying sound of the rain as it falls upon my roof, the gutters, the yard, and the woods behind us, the pictures in my mind reminded me of the numerous times that I have been blinded by what I've seen. My basement is filled with pages and pages of lab results, radiology reports, insurance-related documents, and invoices from the numerous providers I've visited over the years. Somewhere in all of that paper is a story but certainly not one I would have foretold at various stages of this journey based upon the information they contain. Most often, I've imagined that I was approaching this train's terminal station, and yet, there has continued to be optional routes to take. Thank God.

I suddenly pictured a scene from a Shakespearean play that I read in college, taking place on the edge of the White Cliffs of Dover. I don't want to pretend that I remember every detail (I wasn't that kind of student), but I recall someone leading a despairing blind man to a field and convincing him he is at the cliff's edge. Despite the lack of misty breeze or crash of breaking waves, the blind man trusts the one leading him. Pleading solitude, he kneels and then takes a suicidal plunge, seeking the end to his life of suffering. The audience knows that the man has merely fallen forward, feinting, but, upon waking, the man ascribes the miracle of survival to the will of the gods. You literary folks know this to be Scene 6 of Act IV of *King Lear*, with Edgar, in peasant's clothing, leading his father, the blind Earl of Gloucester, to the safety of the Dover countryside. Regardless, it hits close to home. I confess there have been a few moments of weakness when I have uttered silently something similar to:


*"O you mighty gods!*

*This world I do renounce, and, in your sights,*

*Shake patiently my great affliction off:*

*If I could bear it longer, and not fall*

*To quarrel with your great opposeless wills,*

*My snuff and loathed part of nature should*

*Burn itself out..."*

The poor Earl. In hindsight, things haven't been so bad for me after all. I feel mostly fine.

So, I'm no longer tracking my test results, other than imaging, which I'm somewhat forced to with my doctor. But labs and such, I'll just wait to worry when a medical professional personally gives me reason to. Otherwise, I'm in danger of fretting a path to doom. I believe there are supernatural wills at work, but they are much more evident in hindsight against real threats than in anxious moments against perceived ones. Walk and trust. I am a blind man being led by One who was once disguised as a peasant, but He isn't leading me to green pastures* to trick me. It is there that I find rest for my weary soul.

Blessings all. CT Scan in 2 weeks...

* Psalm 23:2

# Vesuvius

## *May 31, 2017*

Greetings folks.

I believe it has been almost five years since my last business trip. If I had to guess, the last was a trip to beautiful Vancouver in 2012, except that it rained the whole time and I spent most of the trip in the convention center. But, since my battle with the "little c" disease began in 2013, there have been no business trips. I attempted one back in 2015, when I was supposed to attend a conference in Berlin, Germany. Kim was coming along with me. She had bought the Fodor's book, researched the castles and other sights that we would enjoy around my attendance at the conference. But, unfortunately, it was not meant to be. Rather than boarding a plane for Berlin, I wound up on a plane to Houston for emergency surgery due to a bowel blockage.

Our flight was scheduled to depart for Berlin on a Tuesday. But, leading up to that trip, I was experiencing severe abdominal pain and other not-so-pleasant symptoms. It got so bad that Kim had to take me to the emergency room. A CT scan at the hospital wasn't definitive for a blockage, though they clearly saw a mass and thought emergency colon resection was the appropriate course of action. As we were already aware of the mass in that area and were under the care of a surgical team at MD Anderson that was monitoring my disease, it was decided that I should instead get a colonoscopy to further diagnose the problem, so the E.R. doctor scheduled it for the following Tuesday, the day we were supposed to fly to Berlin. We moved the flight to Thursday, still hoping we could go, because my doctors believed it unlikely that I was in a life-threatening situation.

Sadly, it was determined that my colon was about 98% blocked by the tumor in my gut, which had grown into and through my colon. I'm still unclear as to why this growth wasn't evident from the CT scans I had been getting up until that time, but, regardless, I had to immediately fly to Houston. So, on the Thursday of our second-chance flight to Berlin, I had surgery at MD Anderson to place a diverting ileostomy on the right side of my belly and was subsequently trained on stoma care and the changing of ostomy bags. I remember well that it was then, while working with the nurse, that I named my new body feature "Vesuvius" because of its penchant for random, loud eruptions.

I'll share one recent story that typifies life with a stoma. A couple of months ago, my daughter, Caroline, and I went to the local cellular retail store to replace the screen cover on her phone. We were the only customers in the store, and we were being assisted by a young woman. Suddenly, as she stood behind the counter, working up the order on her computer, my unruly friend made a sound like "ptttttthhhhhh-bletha-bletha-bletha-bletha-dadada."

You see, Vesuvius can make some strange noises. Embarrassing noises. Noises similar to but shockingly different from those of the bodily efflux of gas with which we're familiar and would suffer almost any pain to avoid emitting in public. At that moment, I probably should have owned it and said, "excuse me!" Another option would have been for me to high-tail it out of there altogether. Instead, I turned to my daughter and said emphatically (though lightheartedly), "Caroline!" and turned back to take in the response of the employee helping us. To her credit, the young woman continued typing as if nothing unusual had happened. My daughter, on the other hand, did an about-face and pursed her lips tightly to stifle her laugh. Her face quivered and tears filled her eyes. I wanted to burst out laughing to relieve the tension. I was mortified, but it was funny. I suspect the employees enjoyed a good laugh at my expense when we were gone.

I bring all of this up because, unless something crazy happens in the next 24 hours, I'll be traveling to Indianapolis this weekend to attend a one-day workshop, and I'm a bit nervous about it. There is no way to predict or prevent the eruptions of Vesuvius, and the noises it makes are definitely not what you want emanating from your body in a room full of strangers at a workshop on software development. Does this sound boring? Perhaps. But I certainly don't want my stoma creating any excitement. I'm hoping and praying that I can survive the workshop without much personal interruption (by eruption).

I'll mention briefly that I return from Indy on Sunday and immediately head to Nashville. I'm getting a CT scan on Monday morning, followed by the usual treatment, presumably. I confess I'm nervous about this too. We hope the trial drugs have continued to be effective against my disease.

We are so thankful for all our friends and family who continue to join us on this journey, in thought, word and deed, particularly the prayers. To those who have shared with me their own hardships, know that we're praying for you too. We're in this together. God bless.

# Latest Results

## *June 6, 2017*

Greetings friends and family,

Kim is driving us home from Nashville. We have been occasionally bringing one of our kids along so they can get an idea of what we experience on our trips, and this time we brought along our Sam, Samantha, whom I call Summer.

Thanks to my dear mother (thanks Mimi!), who helps us afford these biweekly trips, our visits to Nashville aren't 100% about cancer; we typically stay in a nice hotel, have a pleasant dinner, and usually have time for a fun breakfast before we go to the clinic. So, we did all of that, except that I had a CT scan at 8am prior to breakfast at the Pancake Pantry.

We went to my appointment at 10:30, first setting Sam up in the pretty atrium of the adjoining hospital. Our doctor was out of town, so we met with her physician's assistant, who delivered the "good news" and the "worrisome news." Here's the gist of it: the primary tumor that we've been tracking showed additional shrinkage. This is very good news, and I think I'm experiencing some improved symptoms as a result. However, they found a "new left upper quadrant reticular nodular infiltrate within the intraperitoneal fat/omentum and new trace ascites worrisome for early carcinomatosis." Huh? As I write that, half of those words are underlined in red squiggles, so not even this dictionary understands these word, so my dazed, initial response was, "are they saying I'm fat?"

You health professionals out there, I'm sure, know what this report is saying, but in layman's terms, it means there is a small, suspicious spot, surrounded by a little fluid, in or near the wall of my upper left abdomen. O….K…. Gulp.

Now, keep in mind, we were aware of the cancer seeding in my abdominal wall, so this wouldn't exactly be new disease, if that is, in fact, what it is. But these unknown and complicated terms didn't stop me from doing a few Google searches. Please don't do that. Upon reading a few articles, I read a particularly discouraging one, and l experienced a small panic attack that lead to an unsteady walk from the waiting room to the treatment chair.

Suffice to say, I won't be rid of my need to live by faith any time soon!

In my chair, awaiting the infusion drugs that will, hopefully, continue to work against my cancer, I read over and over the CT scan report. After all of the specific details, there are 2 short sentences that summarize the findings. Point 1 offers the promising news, while point 2 required a refill for my anti-anxiety medicine. This is just the cold data that the powerful machines, for which I'm obviously very grateful, provide, though it's strange that radiologists seem comfortable with words like "worrisome" and "suspicious", but I don't remember ever reading words like "encouraging."

It was left to my wife and my infusion nurse to provide some larger, more hopeful perspective. Kim, before taking Sam around Nashville, reminded me of the words of wisdom, no, truth, that was given to this weak worrier back in 2013 by a friend who was visiting me in the hospital after my initial surgery: "the doctors do what they do, and the people of God do what we do. And we pray. And continue to pray."

After Kim had left, I shared with my nurse, Kelly, about the scan results. She first essentially gave me the standard, not-so-helpful comment about "not worrying about it" (!), but then she added something along the lines of "the medical people do what they do, and praying people do what they do."

She had my attention.

She shared with me what she considers to be a miraculous story about a friend of hers who has survived 10 years with stage IV breast cancer against all odds. It was deeply personal to her and undoubtedly one that showed the hand of God, but it didn't hit me particularly hard. But, upon returning to her tasks, she left me with, "God's not done with you yet."

If I nearly fainted upon hearing the latest news and reading about "median survival rates" from an internet article, I can best describe what I felt then as a surge of faith as I fought back tears and remembered God's mercy to me, not just these past four years, but my entire life. God's been with me, and He's not through with me.

To all my friends and family, near and far, who are hurting or lost, I wish for you to hear those words, too. I wish we could make a pact with each other that we won't give up on ourselves or each other. God's not through with us. Let's help each other make this time worthwhile.

Blessings all.

# Red Carpet

## *June 17, 2017*

Greetings friends and family,

Last night, as the evening came to an end, I asked my oldest daughter if she knew about the expression "rolling out the red carpet." She didn't, which surprised me given all the time she spends looking at memes and the like on various social media sites. I had asked her because I used the expression earlier when I had bravely (or was it naively) attempted to offer some advice to my soon-to-be high school daughter.

The genesis of this post was a situation of awkward and presumptuous teenage social dynamics. At a large gathering, my daughter saw other girls exchange whispers and cast suspicious glances her way, which bothered her. She felt judged and rejected. Is this more common with girls? I'm not sure, but I've certainly heard many stories about my daughters being rejected by the indirect but probably benign miscommunication of body language. My advice last night? "Next time you see these girls, greet them warmly, sincerely. Always be willing to roll out the red carpet to allow others to enter your life."

"Huh?"

Then I explained what the expression meant, how we should always welcome people, desire reconciliation of conflict, actual or perceived, slight or grave. That it is good to practice self-giving love.

That advice now rings hollow. I recognize it as oversimplified dogma. Dad-speak. But to my daughter's credit (or perhaps just to get away), her response was music to my parental ears: "OK, Dad." And that was it with her.

Left alone though, it almost felt like I had told her a lie. A voice inside repeated, "get the plank out of your own eye." You see, there are a few people for whom I don't want to roll out the red carpet. Not anymore. I'm tired of being rejected. For them I keep the red carpet tightly wound.

This spring, I spent a week with my family in Washington DC. The obvious attraction is the Mall and surrounding area. We had enjoyed the experience of visiting museums, monuments, buildings of government, the beauty of the expanse of park-like surroundings, and even the solemnity of a national cemetery; all testaments to man's seemingly limitless capacity for good and evil. But it was the walk to the White House that I picture today. To get to it from the Washington Monument, we had to make our way beyond the buildings surrounding the Mall, walk across an out-of-place, unkempt open field, like a wilderness in the middle of civilization. We were then paraded across a pedestri-an-only road, secured, gated and buzzing with security guards. We stepped onto a border of lush, green grass into a crowd of people gaping through the iron fence surrounding the property and separating us from the manicured landscape and the awe-inspiring, historical home of presidents and their families. Unable to enter because we lacked the necessary credentials, I none-theless wished someone would have opened the gate to let us in.

And here's the turn. I now imagine, instead, that I stand at the fence surrounding the mysterious place called Paradise. But instead of being locked out, there is free access. The gate is wide open. The red carpet is rolled out. Not like some tourist-attraction, but somehow just for me. And for anyone. And yet, it feels guarded. I'm wary. I want so much to reach the destination but do-ing so requires acknowledging the way. I can't look past the path. There is a red carpet, and it is welcoming, but I sense that to walk upon it will be to tread upon some-one's life. And as I step, I see that my footprints remain, as if impressed in fresh concrete, but the color is not gray and lifeless but the unmistakable red from a very precious dye.

Oh Jesus, what you have done.

Life always offers many possibilities. With mine, I can attempt to contribute to the work of mankind, perhaps even to have my achievements preserved in a museum or monument, though that's extraordinarily unlikely. I'm more apt to camp out or, perhaps, become stranded in some wilderness. Occasionally, I just like to stick around for the party. Regardless, I often hang back in the crowd, choosing not to walk the narrow way. I sometimes take a few steps in faith, only to turn back time and again.

But the red carpet remains. Well-worn and perfect. Daring me to cross.

Oh man, will we ever reach a place of rest where we can all enjoy life together?

# Celebrating Death?

## *June 25, 2017*

*What did Jesus say to the headwaiter at the Last Supper? 'Separate checks, please.'*

– Edward Abbey

Yesterday was one of those "I'm not going to let cancer slow me down" kind of days. I've been painting my oldest daughter's bedroom, and I'm realizing that 1) I don't think I'm very fast and 2) it can wear you out. But I was hell-bent on putting the first coat on her walls yesterday. And afterwards, the plan was to head to downtown Athens for AthFest for some dinner and to let our kids experience a little Drivin' N Cryin'.

Alas, after I had finished and cleaned up my equipment, I felt dizzy. I started getting the chills. I thought I might be getting a fever. But as my daughters and my wife were ready to leave, I didn't want to ruin their fun. And I didn't want to miss out on any fun with my family. I was determined to go. But I felt like I should check my temperature, just in case, and discovered that I was running a fever approaching 101°. Okay, so that's not very high, but it is when you're on cancer treatment.

Oncologists don't like fevers. But, I figured I was just exhausted and simply needed refreshment, so I got in the car and we drove downtown.

We met my oldest at Ted's Most Best pizza, sat down together, enjoyed some conversation and good food, and I thought I might be getting better. About 30 minutes before Kevin Kinney and company were set to go on stage, I decided to check my temperature again, and it was 101. Ugh. Frustrated, I left my family to go home and rest.

So that's when this post started, at home with a temperature, so that should explain the fever of it.

Yesterday at church, our pastor gave a very helpful sermon, but I won't get into all the details. What I will say is that, interestingly, he ended it by focusing on what we call The Mystery of Faith: "Christ has died, Christ has risen, Christ will come again."

He discussed each in turn, but I couldn't stop thinking about the first part, Christ's death. How is this mysterious? What captivated me then and does so now is the fact that this is the most important death ever. And why is that? On the surface, it seems the second and third parts are the key concepts to Christians, while the first can be taken for granted, since, obviously, everyone dies. Our hope is in the resurrection and the complete redemption of the world. That's the good news, the Gospel. And yet, we start with "Christ is dead," because we know this death was unique among the many billions of human deaths ever. This death is personal for each of us. And we affirm this when we profess faith by proclaiming, "Christ died on our behalf."

Consider for a moment if a family member or a friend jumped in front of a bullet for you. Not only preserving, it would change your life forever. You would never forget that person. You would honor their family. And you would likely seek to live a life worthy of the cost. This was the point of the ending scenes of *Saving Private Ryan*, when James Ryan, gray with years, visits the grave of Captain John Miller, who, along with the rest of their company, had lost his life rescuing Ryan. Ryan drops to his knees to speak directly to his long-gone friend, "I hope that, at least in your eyes, I've earned what all of you have done for me." But this was only for the benefit of one man and his family. With Christ, we believe He essentially stepped in front of a bullet for each of us.

To think about it another way, imagine a gathering of God's people sitting around a table, having enjoyed the feast of life but fretting the forthcoming bill that each lacks the means to pay. The bills, of course, list every one of our transgressions, the self-serving thoughts, words, and deeds. The headwaiter enters the room and asks the table, "Will this be all together? Or separate checks?". I think Edward Abbey's satirical quote (above) is somewhat accurate. But I hear the voice of Jesus silence the din with the astonishing response, "Separate. But bring them all to me." Picture this for all of God's people, and it's an absurd quantity of bills, plastic check trays stacked to the heavens.

Conceptually, it certainly would be easier, so would it make any difference to the outcome if He had said "all together?" If Christ had died for all sin as a whole? It makes all the difference in the world. He acknowledges the sins of each of us and pays each bill separately. With His life. This was an extraordinarily personal event that should bring us to our knees in gratitude and cause us to seek a life worthy of it, but, unlike the burden Captain Miller places on Private Ryan when he says with his last words, "James, earn this. Earn it," only faith is required.

And here we reach a chasm. We don't believe in death, we accept it as fact, so, sure, Christ died. But to believe that He rose three days later requires something other than fact, because resurrection isn't a normal human experience, although His resurrection is one of the most documented events in ancient history. The bridge across the chasm from acceptance of His death to belief in His resurrection is faith, and because Christ died for each of His people individually, each person must find their own way. Separate checks, separate bridges. Mine is like a foot-bridge at a theme park, wobbly and eliciting fear and uncertainty, when, in reality, it is entirely secure. But many don't see it at all. Maybe, like

*Indiana Jones and The Last Crusade,* as he reaches the abyss preventing him from reaching the cave of the Holy Grail, with these blog posts I'm trying to cast a little sand on the bridges of my friends and family so they can see them, but the first step is always ours alone.

Once gripped, it is faith that gives us hope that we too might be resurrected. That we can suffer through any trial because some day all things will be made right, even if it takes a thousand millennia. That's life on the other side, persevering in the hope of the risen Christ. For me, I'd rather live there, even if foolishly wrong, then stay on the side of death, where from dust I was made and will return, and that's the end of my story. Where's the thrill in that? Where's the suspense? No. Much more than merely dust, I sense the soul, a thing created for eternity. It is no less mysterious than what we proclaim: Christ has died, Christ has risen. Christ will come again. Amen.

# Happy 4th, 2017

## *July 4, 2017*

Greetings folks and Happy 4th of July.

I am sitting on the porch, drinking coffee, and enjoying the general feeling of freedom that a national holiday provides. Perhaps in a small way it's also related to what this particular one is about.

I have just finished some time in prayer, and often, as I close my eyes and listen to the sounds of the morning, I remember to be thankful. This morning, the air is heavy with fog, and the songs of the nearby birds seem far off. There's a Sunday morning stillness like the world is sleeping in.

We have just returned from our biweekly trip to Nashville for my treatment. This one was pleasantly uneventful. We took our youngest, Owen, with us, so now all of our children have experienced the thirty or so hours of fun. There's about twelve hours of driving, including stops, four hours or so of dining in a nice restaurant or hanging out in the hotel lobby, ten hours of time in our room, including sleep, and around six hours at the clinic. This is a typical trip when there are no tests. On test days we lose a couple of hours of fun. But this is our general routine, and it has been good for the kids to experience it and for us to get one-on-one time with them, although when I'm at the clinic, Kim takes the kids for something more exciting than what a hospital has to offer. Yesterday, I received a picture of an arms-outstretched Owen in what must have been the central area of Dave and Buster's. Because he is looking up, you can't see it, but I know he's got his game face on, if you know what I mean. They had fun. The kids have a great mom.

Two brief stories from my time in the chair. First, I reported previously about having to collect a day's worth of urine because of an elevated amount of protein that they found in a sample. Well, for the second trip in a row, they saw the same elevated level, but, as the sample was taken in the morning, the nice, but quiet and well-mannered, fifty-something research nurse allowed me to consume copious amounts of water and take the test again. And, fortunately, this time as last, the protein level, now diluted, fell to within the acceptable range, allowing me to avoid taking home a large, orange jug, stealthily carrying it from the refrigerator to the bathroom and back, and explaining, "that's not lemonade."

Second, part of my treatment regimen, along with the infusion in the clinic, is to take two pills a day for three consecutive weeks of an experimental drug, followed by a week off. As this medicine is provided through a clinical trial, I have to return the used cartons, along with a log that tracks when I took the pills each day. The drugs come in boxes with 7 days of medicine. For each day, there are three pills, each in its own clear plastic blister, sealed with thin foil. When I first began the trial, I was taking all three of the pills, but that was making me ill with side effects, so the doctor reduced the dose. So now, I pop out two of the three pills from the column for each day.

I think subconsciously, and, ok, often consciously, I refuse to accept that this battle with cancer is my routine. I pop out two pills a day, yes, but when I do, I send a message to someone somewhere by removing them in random fashion; there's an unused pill each day, but there isn't a straight row of them at the end of the week. If someone is counting the unused pills, I figure they most likely must use a finger and count out-loud. Yesterday, when I received my new box of medicine for the next cycle, the aforementioned composed nurse said, with her calm demeanor, "I just love how you pop out the pills in random order. I thought, 'he's messing with us,' and I just smile. 'That's his way of being defiant to this whole thing.'" She nailed it. Defiance with a smile. I took special pleasure in hearing that I was the only one who did such a thing.

As we drove home yesterday, we passed through the tree-covered mountains, rolling hills, and sweeping farms from Nashville through the rural South back to

**278**

Athens. I tried to picture these surroundings in a dystopian, post-apocalyptic future. Maybe, with our environment under threat and the reportedly chaotic, if not oppressive, rule of people the world over, it might happen some day. But with the seemingly endless green of the countryside just off the interstate, it's hard to imagine a "Divergent" reality. But with the news I receive via the emails, texts and phone calls about friends and families hurting, as the houses pass I can't help but wonder what difficulty is being endured in these homes set in such bucolic surroundings. And when I'm home and I stand at the sink in our mudroom, above which is a cork-board of cards from Christmases past, and recall how much has happened to too many of those families of then smiling faces, I recognize that the real dystopia is behind doors, hardships with unique addresses. And sometimes the only thing that keeps us going are cookies, casseroles, and conversation. Loving and being loved by our neighbors. Persevering together. Today is a day when a lot of folks get together. Let's make the best of it. The fireworks blast again!

If you'll excuse me, I must go pop a couple of pills out of my new box of experimental medicine. Who knows what these drugs will do to me long term. But isn't that the blessing? Long term? I thank the Lord that I'm still here, because, after all, the odds were against it. This go around, instead of randomly popping the blisters across the columns of days, I'm going to make a picture. I think I can pull off a pretty good smile.

Blessings all. Have a great fourth.

# Mayonnaise

## *July 21, 2017*

Greetings folks,

I had my first ever massage yesterday. More specifically, it was a therapeutic massage, which, at least in my mind, makes it markedly different from what I expect one gets on a cruise, at a resort, or otherwise at any place referred to as a "spa". I have intentionally *not* gotten a massage as a matter of principle, like my avoidance of mayonnaise, visiting the Big Apple, and watching *Gone with the Wind*. I have to take a stand somewhere, and, in general, I'm really not into a stranger's hands on me. But, chronic back pain, edema, and other aches and pains point to issues with posture, circulation, and overall muscle tightness. These issues could be due to physical activity (or lack thereof), the impact of surgeries, and even the side-effects of the "therapeutic" drugs that I've received the past four years, and they have turned me into an old man in middle-aged clothing.

Well. You know that feeling you have after you get your teeth cleaned and you almost don't want to eat anything (and certainly avoid coffee) because you want to preserve the smooth, fresh feel of your teeth and gums? This is how I felt about my back when I got home. I didn't want to use it. I wanted to simply lie on the couch and knead the muscles of my back and thighs, remembering that they were meant to be soft and supple when not in use. Instead of having what feels like overcooked pork tenderloins running down my spine, my back muscles were flat and relaxed. Thank you SO much to the therapist at Hand to Sole Reflexology & Massage (Facebook) for the incredible experience. Professional, reassuring, and definitely effective. I left feeling like I had taken a three-hour afternoon nap, flushed and disoriented (in a good way).

So now I've had my first massage. I think I might make it to New York City next year for Owen's 13th birthday (a family tradition). Maybe Kim will get me to watch *Gone with the Wind*. But I won't ever eat mayonnaise, if I can avoid it. And don't try to deceive me by calling it "aioli" or any other fancy word for mayo (rémoulade anyone?), and you can keep the Zaxby's sauce or the thirty Keba sauces not named "Keba sauce" (that one is yogurt-based, in case you're interested).

I'll finish with this. The massage therapist had sent me her address via instant message, and I plugged the address into Google maps and let my car guide me there. As I approached the city, I knew exactly where I was headed, to what was formerly a small home only about a quarter-mile from downtown. It also used to be the photography studio of a friend of mine (shameless plug for the Known Project), and it was there, just under four years ago that a group of faithful Christian men laid their hands on me and prayed for me after I discovered that the cancer that we had hoped had been eliminated had returned. And here I was, returning to that same house to have my first massage, to have hands laid on me again. Just another almost imperceptible reminder of God's work and love. The lightest yet strongest of hands, always on me.

That night in 2014 with those trusted men around me, I remember Pastor Don asking me if there was something specific they should pray for, and I had answered that "I'd stay on the path to cure." Well, doctors don't talk much about cure when it comes to chronic cancer and we're still in the midst of the fight for my life, but, in the immortal words of the aged peasant in *Monty Python and the Holy Grail* as he lay upon a pile of deceased folks to be carted away, "I'm not dead yet." I have no idea what the future holds, but I've survived long enough to see the world with ever-renewing eyes. Perhaps someday I'll be cured of something even more sinister than cancer: doubt.

Just FYI, after a family vacation to a dude ranch Wyoming next week, I'll return to a battery of tests to see where things stand on the cancer front. As always, we treasure your prayers as we pray for you guys too.

Blessings all.

# The Color Orange

## *July 31, 2017*

I always tell people that my happy place is by a river fly-fishing. Often, when I get anxious, stressed out, fearful, I imagine myself standing in shallow water, balancing myself on slick, slimy rocks, casting a fly into a riffle, hoping to see a fish rise. I've been on many fishing trips away from my family over the years, but I had been waiting for the time when I could bring them out west with me, to Montana or Wyoming in particular, to en-counter the natural wonder of the place and perhaps, even, to experience fly-fishing in one of the many, large, picturesque rivers. Well, last week was the opportunity. We took a vacation to a dude ranch just south of Jackson, Wyoming. It is called the Spotted Horse Ranch, and, though the main focus wasn't to be fishing, it was an option, and my kids would finally see what all the fuss has been about. In addition, my brother came, my sister and her family, my mother (the benefactor) and her significant other.

Staying at the ranch struck a great balance between a private vacation and a resort or hotel stay. There were around 35 guests, including us, and many kind staff members, from wranglers to housekeepers and kitchen help. But, though I could tell early on I would see the same people daily, I had intended to keep my health situation private. I wanted to escape, as best I could, from the heaviness of life, especially from conversations about cancer. Well, that didn't last long, as my wife, Kim, told one of the women she had just met about our battle. So, on the second night there, I stood on the deck watching my son attempt to cast a fly into the river that ran beside the ranch, and I wind up in the very type of conversation I had hoped to avoid with the husband. And this is what made it even worse: they were Clemson fans.

Let me say that I don't want this blog to be about the things I don't like. I realize the previous post described my disdain for mayonnaise, but I have to admit that I also hate the color orange. I've been raised to. As a Georgia Bulldogs football fan and geographically surrounded by orange-clad rival teams at Florida, Auburn, Tennessee, Clemson, you can't help it. But honestly, is there anything humanly natural about the color orange? With the Bulldogs, I associate the color red with the blood of life. With these other teams, I regard the followers as fruits. And there were 15 of them in a large, extended family at the ranch. Kids running around everywhere (and I mean running, like cross-country), and I think all they packed in their suitcases were orange shirts bearing the Clemson paw print.

My daughter, Samantha, referred to this group as the

"fit family" because they exercised daily. And often. Not exactly what I consider a relaxing vacation, but impressive. I'll add here that the presence of the many male children was a God-send for my son, Owen, who had playmates during the breaks between organized activities. But there was something else they did. They had family devotionals on the front porch in full view of all of us dudes. This family was certainly disciplined. But we discovered that they were kind, and fun, and sincerely interested in us. They gave off light, and I suspect this is why Kim felt comfortable telling them our story. I confess to being convicted by my desire to escape the world I know, while this family seemed to invite others into theirs.

The trip was amazing. Horse-back rides across rolling mountains to breathtaking views. Whitewater rafting. Cookouts. A rodeo. And, yes, fly-fishing. But each activity brought a sense of longing with the pleasure. I couldn't get close enough to Grand Teton mountain, even atop its neighbor, Rendezvous, at 10,000 feet. The rapids were thrills for mere moments. I didn't catch the 25" trout that has eluded me for 20-plus years of fly-fishing. We even left the rodeo early. But we have memories for a lifetime, pictures and video to remember what we did and who we were with. Priceless, really, though my mother's American Express card says otherwise.

But the trip also took a toll. I may have wanted to escape the attention of being a cancer survivor, but my body didn't stop reminding me. My recent issue with edema in my right leg reached a peak of its own on Saturday night, as I was swollen from my hip to my toes, as if I had stepped into a nest of yellow jackets. Now THAT would have been fitting, considering those annoying bees are the mascot of another of Georgia's bitter rivals, Georgia Tech. I lay on my bed that night, leg resting on a stack of orange pillows. I couldn't escape a thing, it seems.

Late to bed Sunday night at home, I awoke early, desiring to pray and read the Bible. My Scripture journal led me to Acts 27, and I read about the apostle Paul's perilous journey across the Mediterranean, Aegean, and Adriatic seas, seeking Rome and audience with Caesar to plead his case. Their ship ultimately wrecked on the island of Malta. But before doing so, Paul was visited by an angel who reassured him that he would indeed make his way to Rome and to Caesar, and Paul likewise encouraged the others on the ship to take heart because the Lord was with them and had promised deliverance to their destination.

Another Summer vacation over, will I hear the voice of an angel promising me another? Are there signs telling me I'll live long enough to see my children graduate high school, college, marry, and make families themselves? Will I ever catch the trophy trout? Have I any promises to cling to?

Well, yes, but not for tomorrow, for eternity. Jesus promised me Himself. The true Happy Place, mysterious, yes, but not ever-eluding. And the orange family are reminders. We have so much more than photos, souvenirs, or other keepsakes with their promises to pray for us and follow our journey by reading my blog. Our family of brothers and sisters in Christ has grown. We, as sojourners in the world but not of it, are proclaimers of the Promise, and we reassure each other that we will reach our destination, find audience with the King, and are safest if we stick together.

For as long as I endure edema, I will need to elevate my leg. Naturally, my resting place is my living room couch and a stack of red pillows. Hereafter, I'll remember the orange ones at the Spotted Horse Ranch and the family with the Clemson clothes. But I get it now. The red of our blood mixed with white light of the Spirit. Orange? Not humanly natural, no, but another reminder of glory? I'll never see that color the same way again.

By the way, have you ever seen a Snake River Cutthroat Trout? I swear they bleed orange....

Thanks for reading. If you've made it this far, we're heading to Nashville for treatment on Aug 2. I have an eye exam to check for any retinal damage and a heart ultrasound to check for heart inflammation, both possible side effects of treatment. And I have a CT scan to assess the state of my disease. As always, we cherish your prayers.

Blessings all. Even you orange people.

# Whack-a-Mole

## *August 3, 2017*

We're back from Nashville, and I figured I should provide an update. I offer humble thanks to those who
read these posts and for those who are praying for us.
I don't want to post too often, but if you write a post
before the tests, you owe it to those who've read to
give an update afterward. Briefly, my eyes and heart
are doing fine, though I may finally be getting some
glasses. As for the disease, I'll just say upfront that my
oncologist said, "the scans look _____."  The word in
the blank is either "great" or "good" depending on if
you ask Kim or me what she said. Regardless, I got up
from my chair and gave the doctor a hug. Suffice to say,
she is very happy with how the treatment is going, so
we all should be too.

Here's a brief summary:  the main tumor is either stable or smaller (great), the node and fluid that were previously described as "worrisome" is not visible on the
current scan (great), but there were new, "tiny" nodes
found in the lungs which are "worrisome" (there's that
word again). So, if we summarize the past 2 scans, and
really, going back years, things show up on a scan that
a radiologist terms "worrisome" but that the oncologist

says "I'm not worried about it" and then you get a new scan and the previously "worrisome" stuff is gone, affirming the oncologist's wisdom in not worrying about it, but you see new "worrisome" stuff and the oncologist again says she's not worried about it, and you're left confused about what is real or a ruse. I know. It sounds like a line from Bilbo Baggins' eleventy-first birthday speech. One doc says worry, another says don't. Scan-to-scan, it's nodal whack-a-mole. No matter how reassuring my oncologist is, one thing's for sure, peace of mind is not something with which I typically leave the clinic after a CT scan.

But, as always, the great story unfolds, offering a change in perspective.

As I sat in the treatment chair yesterday, an older gentleman with a walker trudged his way into the adjacent chair. There only to receive fluids to improve his well-being, he moaned and grunted frequently, eyes pinched closed from neck and back pain. Kim and I were very concerned for him. His nurses were, too, and they encouraged him to go to the hospital for care. He refused, and, when the IV bag was empty, asked for his walker, stood, gathered himself, and left to drive himself home. I assume he made it, though I'm sad that he's alone, and I think it's dangerous that he's on the road.

On the way home, Kim asked, "when do you just give up?" She was speaking specifically in regard to this man, but I heard it as rhetorical, so, after a pause, I replied, "never." It came out weakly, though, my mind attempting to signal my tired body with the reminder that the sun would rise in the morning, as would I. For Kim, the scan results are definitely great news, as there doesn't appear to be any immediate threat to my life. Now almost a year into the third treatment protocol, Kim is thrilled with what she might consider "bonus time" in this long-term game of whack-a-mole, gaining life with every new day. I still struggle with exhaustion from wielding the whack-hammer, thinking about the life that might be lost if the "worrisome" stuff progresses to real concern. And there lies a critical difference in outlook, one for which I'm so glad my wife reminds me. How I live, my attitude, not only affects the quality of my life but also how my body responds to what I'm very comfortable in calling a fight. Medically speaking, stress causes inflammation, and inflammation is unhealthy.

As most of you probably know, Senator John McCain was recently diagnosed with a brain tumor. There was an outpouring of support, of course, but a common theme was that his tumor was up against a strong foe, a veteran of battles of various types, well prepared for this new challenge. However, I read an opinion article on CNN.com[1] that argues that cancer is not a "war, fight, or battle." While I agree on some points, I definitely think that attitude, when facing cancer or any chronic disease for that matter, is critical. It is a fight, and we have to arm ourselves physically, mentally, and spiritually, especially in those moments when we might consider giving up. So, while I wish my aged treatment neighbor had accepted medical assistance instead of slumping into the driver's seat of his car, I appreciate his will to fight. Onward we battle.

As I've written before, I don't practice thinking positively, I believe in living eternally. So, I hope you'll excuse me as I go to my Happy Place. A place I know I can find peace of mind. But first I'll arm myself with Saint Patrick's Breastplate.

> *"... Christ with me, Christ before me, Christ behind me,*
>
> *Christ in me, Christ beneath me, Christ above me,*
>
> *Christ on my right, Christ on my left,*
>
> *Christ when I lie down, Christ when I sit down, Christ when I arise..."*

Amen.

1 CNN Opinion: http://www.cnn.com/2017/07/21/opinions/cancer-is-not-a-war-jardin-opinion/index.html

# Pulp Fiction

## *August 21, 2017*

A few weeks ago, we had a dinner party at our house, and, as we sat around the table of our pizza garden, one of our friends spoke of a YouTube video she had seen where a man, Mark Gungor, described the differences between men's and women's brains. I laughed as I watched, but I am pretty sure he's serious, though I'm not sure about the science behind it. But according to Mark, a key difference is how men and women both organize our thoughts, in what he describes as a network of "thought boxes." He speaks while pacing around an empty stage, save two pedestals upon which rest models of human brains, one male and the other female. He begins by explaining that men are generally able to focus primarily on particular boxes (specific areas of their lives), while with women, the relationships between the different boxes are critical. Because of this, he claims, men are capable of maintaining a completely empty box, thereby allowing them to enter a state essentially devoid of thought. As he stood over the man's brain, he jokingly described the lounging man, mindlessly killing time. And then, he approached the woman's brain, he makes the sign of the cross as he hesitatingly described the complex thinking of women and how they are always processing many things at once.

Since our friend told us about Mark Gungor's theories and having watched the video, I've spent a fair amount of time reflecting upon it (shocker). I spent a weekend at a monastery last year, and I experienced a little about the monastic life. As I understand it, monks spend a lot of time in quiet solitude, not thinking, but emptying their minds. I don't know, but do nuns spend long periods in silence like that? My preconceived notions say no, picturing nuns as always busy. Like my wife. So, perhaps there is some truth to what Mark says, but, honestly, I can't relate. My thought boxes are either inseparably interconnected or their contents chaotically disorganized like a junk drawer.

Forgive me for the unsanctified reference, but I picture a scene in the Quentin Tarantino film *Pulp Fiction*, where Butch Coolidge, played by Bruce Willis, stands at the door of a pawn shop. He has just escaped from its basement after being beaten but before having to endure the most inhumane of torture. Down the stairs he has just ascended, though, is Marsellus Wallace (Ving Rhames) who was captured along with him, and he is now being disturbingly assaulted. Bruce pauses for a moment, and then, shockingly, forgoes his freedom in order to return to the basement to save the man, a gangster who had been trying to kill Butch. But to rescue him, Butch needs the perfect weapon. This being a pawn shop, there are many options. He circles the room quickly, testing the wieldiness of a hammer, a bat, and a chainsaw. Then, as he scans for a better weapon, his eyes freeze on an item high up on a wall, and the camera turns to share what he has found. A Samurai sword. This is the one. Personal and deadly. Suffice to say that he unsheathes the sword and descends the stairs to rescue one enemy and slay others.

I recalled this scene because I often replay imaginary arguments until I find the perfect words with which to end them. But, ultimately, despite the din of discord, at some point I hear a voice reminding me of who I am. I'm a Christian. I shouldn't humble friends nor enemies with my own power but should humble myself because of a love that is conquering my heart and has won my soul. And my only hope is that personal humility and vulnerability might in some way be a positive influence on others in whom that same love is also at work. And when I recognize my pride expressing itself, my only recourse is to pray, attempt to empty my mind, and then focus on the things for which I should be thankful, not resentful. But this is easier said than done, because it's me in the pawn shop, either searching its contents looking for the perfect solution for my problems or those of a loved one or stuck in the basement, kidnapped by dark thoughts.

How easy it was for Mark Gungor to describe thought boxes as he peered down into the model brains containing them. And, no offense to monks, perhaps the monastic life naturally creates an order and simplicity apart from the worldly chaos in which it is so easy for me to get lost. Having been stuck in a place of irrational discontent, it's more accurate to picture myself inside one of those boxes, a junk drawer of life stuff, my disease and my longevity, my wife and children, finances and job, the house, and the ever-present relational difficulties with or between family and friends. As I find with the drawers in my house that are organized occasionally but are destined for the label "miscellaneous", in moments of confusion, not only are my thoughts jumbled, I feel overwhelmed by the various things that I cannot control, and suddenly even small problems seem an enormity. I don't see any thought boxes; I'm part of the junk in one. The more I try to control my life, the more frustrated I get, either wanting to overpower my problems or, sometimes, just give up. The only solution is if there is something outside of me to maintain control for me. Ultimately, to save me.

It cuts my heart deeply to admit this. It cuts to have to embrace it daily. I need a savior, and He must wield love. It's the only way.

I imagine God, instead of Mark Gungor, peering down into my brain and observing my vain efforts to compartmentalize things, to manage so-called thought boxes. Regardless of the difference between how men and women think, I think the idea of an empty box is ultimately pointless. The closest I want to be to emptiness is a quiet beach with a distant horizon where, even alone, I feel the strange comfort that can only be explained by the presence of God.

So where am I now?  A year ago, I'll confess, I was in a very difficult place, coming off of the failed surgery. These days, I feel much more myself and free, but I'll never forget the times of darkness. I don't ever want to go back there, but I live with some fear that an un-expected disaster, a late-night phone call from a friend or family-member, or a "worrisome" CT scan will send me down the path of frustration, anxiety and even to despair, trapped again inside my own mind.

So, in my version of *Pulp Fiction*, the pawn shop scene takes place in one of my cluttered thought boxes. Suit-ably, I have some experience, at least mentally, with being both a proud villain and a tortured prisoner, but here I picture myself as Bruce Willis's flawed hero. I don't relate to Tarantino's glorification of power, though, because experience has shown that no weap-on restores order or truly frees. When I find myself searching through the junk for instruments of rescue, my eyes can't fall upon the sword, they must rest upon the cross. I'm sure I can find one in a pawn shop. And when I do, like any other magical moment when God is found, my face will daze with awe and wonder.

Blessings all

# Granola

## *August 30, 2017*

I learned something this week. I probably shouldn't eat granola, especially when it contains sunflower seeds or other nuts. But before I get into this, I should say that I was hesitant to provide this update, thinking it may be a bit too personal. But wait. Too personal? The other voice in my head reminds me that I probably cannot get more personal than I have already, but still, it seems strange to share a story about a little bump in the road. At some point, as those who've been following for a while know, I started using this blog in large part to talk about life in general (the "two stories" stuff) as opposed to the "my arm hurts when I move it like this" stuff. But as Kim reminded me (again) this morning, these things are all related, and there's an ebb and flow to what I feel led (or called) to share here.

Sunday night was a fun one in Nashville, as the treatment trips go. It sounds smug to say this, but I got a great rate at the Hermitage hotel, and so Kim and I slept in style that night. And it was just that night, because my treatment appointment was at 8am Monday morning. We arranged for room service for 6:45, and I, not wanting to pay $20 for dry, lukewarm eggs, decided on a bagel and the yogurt with granola. Some of you may recall that I spent four nights in the hospital about eight months ago due to a small bowel obstruction, but I haven't had any issues since, though I've been careful about what I eat and try to chew my food well. The only thing I avoid, at this point, are raw vegetables, otherwise I've been eating normally (mayonnaise aversion aside). My pen hovered, though, over the yogurt offering, wondering if I was OK to eat the granola.

Answer to that question: No.

I'll just state simply, if embarrassingly, that when I arrive home on Monday evenings after treatment, I typically have to empty "the bag" (if you aren't familiar with what I'm talking about, see the previous post "Vesuvius"). But Monday night, the bag was basically empty, and this was a big warning sign. It wasn't long before I began experiencing extreme abdominal pain and spent the night in bed or the bathroom, resolute that I was NOT going to a hospital. I survived, though the "sleep insight" as reported from my Fitbit depicts a rough night. Tuesday was a day of recovery, but I hoped to join my 12-year old son, Owen, that evening for his first junior golf league match, which I did.

And here's where the time of self-pity began. First, ordinarily, I would *never* obtain a cart for myself to follow my son as he walks a golf course, my obstinate mind associates a weakness for such acts (or at least an agedness), but because of the fear of leg edema, I sheepishly gave the man in the golf shop $10 in order to ride the six holes. Second, Vesuvius was erupting, and the bag was filling up rapidly as my body continued its process of recovery, which includes my form of diarrhea and is unpleasant, especially around strangers. And third, I received a call, on the first hole, from a nurse from Tennessee Oncology telling me that my lab work indicates that I have hypothyroidism, a common side effect of immunotherapy, and I would need to begin a regimen of medication to combat it. Ugh.

(queue the violins, please.)

All of this is hidden from people that don't know me, and, honestly, even from those who do. If there were outward signs of such handicaps (kudos if you caught that), people would naturally understand my need to prop a leg, need to be near real restrooms (with plumbing, TP, and soap), and hesitancy to do manly activities that healthy middle-aged men should do to show that they still have copious amounts of testosterone flowing through their veins. But when all of your ailments are hidden beneath your clothes and you otherwise appear healthy, then an expectation follows. Or perhaps friends and family have an honest desire to help me live life to the fullest, assuming that what is holding me back is mental; and sure, some of it is.

This week is the start of college football, and UGA has a 6pm home game Saturday, with plenty of time to tailgate, since it isn't one of the hated 12pm kickoffs (but which made it easy for me to handle). So as my son is counting down the days ("3 days, dad!"), I feel the pressure (and desire) for a fun afternoon on my feet, but I dread the silent fatigue and frequent trips to the porta potties. At some level I don't care what others might think, but disappointing my kids absolutely crushes me.

(are the violins still playing?)

It's Wednesday, and I'm getting my strength back, system returning to normal. As I sat on the porch while the kids got ready for school, I thought to myself how I needed some time in prayer and the Word. My patient wife, though, picked up a book (a gift from our dear friends, James and Susan) with which many of you are familiar, *Morning and Evening: Daily Readings*, by Charles Spurgeon. I find these devotions hit-or-miss, though, sometimes lacking, for me, a personal touch that gets to my heart. I often picture him standing on a soapbox, so to speak, preaching at me, but other times the brilliance for which he is famous shines. As she pulled the book back to read aloud, I said something along the lines of, "C'mon Spurgeon, hit me in the heart." (I asked for it...)

"August 30: Wait for the Lord. — Psalm 27:14".

The whole devotion is worth reading, but this is what really got my attention:

> *There are hours of perplexity when the most willing spirit, anxiously desirous to serve the Lord, knows*

*not what part to take. Then what shall it do? Vex itself by despair? Fly back in cowardice, turn to the right hand in fear, or rush forward in presumption? No, but simply wait. Wait in prayer, however. Call upon God, and spread the case before Him; tell Him your difficulty, and plead His promise of aid. In dilemmas between one duty and another, it is sweet to be humble as a child, and wait with simplicity of soul upon the Lord. It is sure to be well with us when we feel and know our own folly, and are heartily willing to be guided by the will of God. But wait in faith. Express your unstaggering confidence in Him; for unfaithful, untrusting waiting, is but an insult to the Lord.*

That last part though.

As she finished, I recalled a time, probably four years ago, where I prayed on my knees to God, vowing that I would endure any amount of suffering but pleading that he would not take my life early. I just cannot imagine my children's lives without me, and the thought strikes me too often, even yesterday as I watched Owen walk to the tee box to hit his drive on hole #2.

How many times can I perform this pirouette? Self-pity to thankfulness? More frequently than I'm comfortable with, it seems.

Am I crazy?

Does anyone out there relate?

*God, please protect me from insulting you with faithlessness. Help me to trust. Help me to be thankful. Help me to enjoy today. Help me to shrug off, if not laugh, the secret side effects of life. In these, I know I'm not alone.*

# Tidal Surge

## *September 21, 2017*

I've certainly shared a bit about the Spring of 2013 when I was first diagnosed with (whisper voice) *cancer*, but I don't believe I've shared much about the life circumstances of that time. Much changed that April, obviously, but it had particular impact on the relationship that my wife and I had with our church community group. At that time, I was leading the group, and I will never forget sitting down with my friends and telling them of my diagnosis. Everyone was very comforting, but from the moment of my uttering the word (again, whisper voice) *cancer*, I could feel the heaviness of the situation. I could sense the gravity-like pull that my news had in the room. I had to step down from leading because of the need for surgery and treatment, so we were absent for most of the remaining meetings. But, community group came to an end that year, so it wasn't as if we had left. But, when it started back the next fall, we didn't return.

A year or so later, we finally attempted to rejoin a community group (a different one), but we found it difficult. Our attendance was sporadic, admittedly, which impeded our ability to form deep relationships, but the bigger issue, at least for me, was the time of prayer. I could feel the familiar gravity as the requests slowly circled the room and my turn drew near. I felt an uneasy combination of power and vulnerability in burdening the group with updates. It was as if the direness of my health issue was sucking from the group the significance of the trials of others. I may have imagined that, but when life-stories of others are qualified with, "But this is nothing compared to what you're going through," it's not surprising that I began to feel uncomfortable and a distraction to these intimate friends doing life together.

So, we stopped attending a community group. We were too often unable to attend the weekly gatherings due to my treatment schedule and it was easier, though not necessarily right, to avoid the awkward "coffin in the room" feelings (see my previous post, "Elephant") that those evenings produced.

Earlier this week, my office neighbor, Mark, leaned into my doorway and asked me why I hadn't posted recently. Slightly surprised by his query, I asked him if he wanted a health update or more of my philosophical and spiritual ramblings. He replied that he wanted to know what was going on in my head. It was then that I recalled a photo, taken prior to Hurricane Irma's arrival, of Tampa Bay residents standing on sand that had only hours before been covered in water, Irma having sucked millions of gallons into its churning engine. The space between the men plays on the Tampa skyline in the background, and, clutching their phones, hands raised to the sky for photos of the impending fury from above, you sense they're aware that something terrible is taking place somewhere and is coming for them but they're unsure of what to do other than to document that they were there when it happened. And this describes how I feel right now. I'm at a place of treatment-mediated peace, and some other crisis has sucked the self-thoughts and self-feelings out of my head and heart, and I'm unsettled about what to do. Dear friends are suffering a category 5 crisis of greater power than I've honestly ever personally experienced. Are my texts, CaringBridge comments, and prayers enough?

Forty or so miles from my home, friends that I've known since high school are dealing with (raised voice now) **childhood cancer** (September is Childhood Cancer Awareness Month). Their 16-year old daughter, Katie, was recently diagnosed with rhabdomyosarcoma, a rare and dangerous cancer. It came upon her seemingly overnight, and she has undergone more harsh treatment and side effects in the past 6 months than I've experienced in the past 4 years. I've endured a steady grind with ups and downs, sure, but she's suffering near constant physical and emotional duress in the short period since diagnosis and that will continue for the next several months until treatment is complete. And her parents. My friends. They have to watch. It hurts me so. We pray that the treatment will be the end of it. Cure.

Knowing what these friends are going through, I don't feel comfortable talking about myself right now, let alone asking for prayer. I feel like a man standing on the soggy seabed with a "sick sense of peace" (thanks, Eric), realizing that, not too distantly, friends' lives are in turmoil, but I'm also wary that the waters of my own troubles will return, perhaps in tsunami force. But, given my familiarity with guilt for being the unwitting winner of the crisis-comparison game, I am sure they must want to be an active part of a community that serves and prays for one another, not live as objects of unreciprocated love.

(I have a CT scan on Monday. There, I said it.)

This past week we gathered with friends from our church for the kickoff of community group for the new year (following the school calendar). There was no Bible lesson that night and no prayer time, it was potluck and fellowship, and it was great. Relaxing. As we left our car and approached the host's house, we heard the sound of children playing in the backyard. It was good music and brought back sweet memories. And it affirmed our motivation for joining this new group, with me as the eldest, I believe — to deepen relationships and come alongside friends as they live through the seasons of life with which Kim and I are now veterans, but also to have our hands on the oars of the small lifeboat in which Christ has placed us, to persevere with our brothers and sisters with Him should the seas get rough. And they will.

Returning to hurricanes, satellite images taken while Hurricane Irma assaulted Florida showed also the slow approach of Jose and the formation of Maria in the east Atlantic. I imagine the players in a classic horror film; the pursued are in a panic to escape while the killer calmly, assuredly follows and nonetheless catches its victims unprepared. In this life, the storm is either raging in our homes, the homes of those we love, or it's coming. Or all of that. Either way, we can't ride the storm out alone. We've got to help each other.

Taking a word from Acts 22:21, the Lord says, "Go!" Sometimes that means hands and feet but other times it is timely encouragement. I know from my own experience the importance of texts, comments, and unbeknownst prayers because they are reminders of being loved and Loved. Whatever it looks like, there's danger in being an awestruck bystander or trapped by one's own circumstances. For the tides of darkness surge under powers outside of our control, mild and extreme, gravity and storm, and it threatens to overwhelm us. There is an ever-present, urgent need to seek Higher Ground.

# Health Update

## *September 26, 2017*

Hey folks

Well, it was a good trip to Nashville. As has happened in the past, previously worrisome stuff is no longer visible (like the potentially suspicious lung nodes). But this time, the radiologist on duty didn't find any new spots suspicious for cancer. Further, the existing stuff that we've been following for years is stable. The short conclusion is "improved/stable with limited evidence of disease." That sounds good, right? As far as we can tell, the treatment continues to work, and the oncology team are all smiles.

These 8-week intervals between CT scans are short. It used to be 3-months. It doesn't seem like much, but it increases the tension a bit. It feels a little like living in the Dharma Initiative hatch with the clock winding down. At regular intervals, alarms start going off. Fortunately, someone enters some data into a system and then we get to relax for a while. And the clock just got reset...whew.

I can't help but share this story. Kim and I stopped for a quick dinner in Dalton, Ga on our way home. While eating, Kim explained that she had deliberately parked a little farther away from the walkway to the restaurant than necessary (which I had tiredly questioned) so we could get some extra steps. Kim lamented that her step-counter only showed around 2100, since we had been sitting all day, first in the clinic and then in the car. I teased that I was beating her, if only by a few hundred steps, wondering if the morning's CT imaging had given me a boost. I had 2,619 steps. At about the same time, I glanced from my booth out the window to see a large sign towering above us from the neighboring gas station, showing their prices. I about spit my food all over Kim when I saw that Regular was $2.61[9]. 26--19, steps and gas. What are the odds of that??

Thank you for your prayers and your consistent, sweet encouragement.

Blessings,

Brent

# The 100ᵗʰ Sheep

## *October 16, 2017*

My mother lives in a beautiful house atop a hill in Dekalb County, a turkey's flight away from where I grew up (turkeys don't fly very far). Thanks to some enterprising folks back in the 1930s and 40s who propagated it around the South to prevent soil erosion, kudzu has taken over these hills, choking the bushes and trees that my mom would prefer to flourish. I wasn't aware that you could do this, but she has rented a small flock of sheep for a short time to graze about her property and clean up the grounds. I take it that they love kudzu.

The sheep are contained by a temporary electric fence to prevent them from wandering. Farmers wanting to make a few extra bucks on those sheep in the pen? Rent them out to refined yet free spirited suburbanites with a few dollars in their account and no fear of reprisals from a homeowner's association. Picturing her sipping wine on her deck, watching the woolen creatures meander about, it's not far-fetched to imagine her acquiring a permanent flock. I know not to expect lamb for any holiday dinners.

It's Tuesday morning, and my mother sent me pictures of the sheep. As cute as they are, my thoughts drift to dark places because I'm agitated. I have just returned from treatment in Nashville, and I always feel this way. Tired and grumpy. A drop (or vial) of self-pity. And the self-pity reminds me that I'm dealing with a condition that I didn't ask for and cannot control, and my mind repeatedly iterates over the friends and family that, frankly, are miserable or are making others so. And I have the answer, right? Jesus, right? I proclaim, proclaim, proclaim, or at least think I do, and expect change, change, change. But some of this misery has lasted a lifetime. The misery *is* the life. And misery is exhausting.

And then I think of mom's sheep. If one were to escape, to get lost in the woods, my mom would drop everything, including her wineglass, and go running after it, though I'm not sure what she'd do if she found it. Lure it back into the fold with a favorite snack, say pretzels filled with peanut butter? Camembert cheese?

Many of you know where this is going. The Bible speaks again!

The parable of the lost sheep (Luke 15:3–7). Such a short and sweet parable about a shepherd of 100 sheep who discovers one is missing. He leaves the 99 that are safe together to pursue the one that has strayed. The parable describes the joy of the shepherd as he brings the lost sheep home, "⁵ And when he has found it, he lays it on his shoulders, rejoicing..." (ESV).

A simple and beautiful image.

But if this is a parable, then the stories are about people, and from my experience, people don't usually think they're lost, and when you pursue someone as such, they don't typically thank you for finding them. In an age when self-reliance is king, who needs a shepherd? Who wants to be a sheep? No one likes to be herded. The lost sheep often escapes and seeks others who don't want to be a part of *that* flock. Pursued by the shepherd, the sheep runs.

How do pastors endure? Even in my own calling to pursue the lost, I see how it affects me. How vulnerable we become, how dangerous it is to be involved in others' lives, especially those who are hurting deeply, or to be entangled in broken relationships. Expanding the parable, I picture the shepherd, staff in hand, staggering over a craggy landscape, calling his sheep by name. The distant bleats that direct his course could be distress, but they may very well be the sound of its joy in its freedom. Upon finding it, does the master lasso and subdue it? Would that be cause for rejoicing upon return? No. I can only picture a scene where the lost collapse under the weight of their own brokenness, and it is then that the shepherd lifts and carries them home on his shoulders. On mornings like Tuesday, I wonder when the shepherd himself collapses in exhaustion and who will be there to rescue him.

As you all know by now, I'm a Christian, and the flock to

which I belong gathers once a week on Sunday mornings. Other than that, it's free time in the pasture. But to a lone sheep struggling with physical, mental or emotional distress in a world that screams your beliefs are foolish or quietly ignores them altogether, the pasture feels more like wilderness, and in it the sheep is lost.

It is now Monday morning, and I'm stuck at home. The past several months I've been battling a wound near my ileostomy, the portion of my small intestine that was exposed on the right-side of my abdomen to divert waste from my colon, which is a dead-end tunnel (a tumor blocks the exit). This is technical, but the wound is in a difficult area to heal because it lies under the appliance (known as a wafer) that I must attach to my body to collect stool (I know, gross). I would normally avoid sharing any of these details with anyone outside my wife and closest friends, but I've had a very difficult weekend and I'm beginning to lose heart. The wound seems to have eroded tissue under the skin, and now a trench forms whenever the stoma contracts, creating an opening under the wafer that allows stool to smother the wound, preventing healing, causing infection. The recommendation is to change the wafer/pouch system every 4-5 days and no fewer than 3, but I think I've changed it 8 times since Friday. It was so painful that night that I "slept" on the couch in the basement, kitty-cornered at the intersection of two sectional modules. I lay on my stomach with the stoma facing down in the open corner of the angle change with a dog waste bag taped around the area instead of the pouch system, hoping to avoid the problems that it causes when I sleep on my back. It wasn't a good look when my wife found me early Saturday morning.

So when I started this post 6 days ago, I had in mind friends and family with which I'm tired from either pursuing or even merely watching as they wander, knowing the misery they cause themselves or those around them. But this morning, I'm exhausted from my body's brokenness and wonder where is my Shepherd to comfort me? Some days are spent in green pastures, others in the valley of the shadow of death.

When does the shepherd triumphantly carry the sheep home on his shoulders? I always picture today. Or tomorrow. Sometime soon, if we just hang on. I imagine the time when relationships are reconciled, when the pain subsides or the injury heals, when the sun comes out on friends stuck in the darkness of debilitating depression, and, I'll say it, when friends and family who live like I, in my weakness, so often believe, that "all you touch and all you see/Is all your life will ever be", finally will themselves to enter a church and join a flock of their own (to borrow a line from Pink Floyd's 'Breathe').

It could be that this is something I'm not meant to see, not on this side of the grave anyway. Perhaps the sheep in the parable are souls, not people. And it is when we die that the Shepherd calls us for the last time. We hear His voice, and we turn to Him–that's what it means to repent, after all. He picks us up and carries us home on His shoulders, and there is joy in Heaven. This Shepherd never tires.

I have made several phone calls the past few days. I've talked to nurses in Houston (MD Anderson Cancer Center) and Nashville (Tennessee Oncology). I've gotten conflicting advice on how to treat the wound. It was suggested that I might have a condition known as *pyoderma gangrinosum*, and I need to see a dermatologist for diagnosis and treatment. A phone call produced an appointment for Tuesday, but, as I had a leak again last night and needed to change the pouch system, I had hoped to get in today so I could change it in the doctor's presence and avoid having to do it again tomorrow, if so fortunate. I then made a call to the wound/ostomy answering service at MD Anderson to clarify if it was better to change the system frequently to keep the wound clean or to keep it covered and avoid the irritation of frequent removal.

I received a call-back 15 minutes later from a helpful nurse who spent several minutes on the phone with me discussing my condition, what I've tried, and her offering suggestions. She didn't solve my problems, but she certainly clarified the situation for me. Before we hung up, I asked for her name. In a world of millions of voices and thousands of faces, names are still important. I didn't want hers for my records, I wanted it because if this life is eternal, there's a chance we may actually meet, and I can thank her personally, pilgrim-to-pilgrim. Names matter, also, if you hope to hear your Shepherd's call. She answered, "Faith. F. A. I. T. H. Faith..... Is there anything else I can help you with?"

I bleated the words "no, thank you" before I put the phone down and cried.

# Living Church: Strength in Weakness

## *November 16, 2017*

Periodically, our church invites members to speak to the congregation about their experiences living by faith, in a segment we call "Living Church." I last spoke about 4 years ago, not long after I had completed the first round of chemotherapy. Recently, Pastor Jared asked me to speak again, this time about "weakness and faith," as part of his sermon series, "God for Us." I agreed, but it made me anxious, as I knew he specifically wanted me to speak on weakness, faith, and cancer. These are subjects I write about often, but to open up personally about such things in front of a hundred or so faces is difficult. And though the song is upbeat, Jared had me speak after the congregation sang a song titled, "From the Depths of Woe"! What an intro. I began by teasing Jared a bit to lighten the mood, though one of my daughters encouragingly described my opening as "awkward."

My favorite all time movie is John Boorman's *Excalibur*. Seen at the age of 12 on HBO (my parents must have been out to dinner), this was my introduction to epic battle scenes and film scores (and other formative elements). As the legend goes, the knights undertake the quest to find the Holy Grail, the chalice shared by Christ at the Last Supper. The knights spend years on the quest, many dying or giving up. The unlikely hero is Sir Perceval, though, his purity and strength of heart enabling him to persevere to the gateway of the sanctum of the Grail, and he happens upon it twice–true near-death experiences. His first opportunity to obtain it arrives while being hanged. In a semi-conscious state, he arrives at a castle, fully armored, sweaty, haggard, cuts and sores on his face, and the grail is within his grasp (that's him in the featured photo). He is asked a riddle from a godly voice and is afraid. He turns and runs. He survives the hanging and lives for a second chance later, when, further ragged, plate mail rusted nearly through, he arrives at a village of medieval squalor. Lacking the will to fight, he is beaten into a river by the peasants and sinks to the bottom of a deep pool under the weight of the armor worn for protection. Drowning, he shakes out of the armor and pulls himself out of the river to suddenly come before God (or Arthur, or Jesus) with the Grail again in his reach. He solves the riddle and brings the Grail to King Arthur to restore him and the land. It is a moving scene, but what I find interesting is that Perceval's body appears totally restored as he approaches the castle. Armorless, shirtless, he looks healthy. He's got a few scrapes, but where are the marks on his neck from his time hanging from a tree? As a survivor of many trials, he's unrecognizable.

**320**

My quest is much less grand: to find purpose. But, like Perceval, have I found it at the weakest point of my life?

Here are the verses on which I reflected (full verses below). Themes: weakness, purpose, conforming to Christ, the question of where belief resides, and living by faith. Is that all?

> *Romans 8:26-30*
> *²⁶ Likewise the Spirit helps us in our weakness...*
> *²⁸ And we know that for those who love God all things work together for good, for those who are called according to his purpose.*
> *²⁹ For those whom he foreknew he also predestined to be conformed to the image of his Son.*
>
>
> *Romans 10: 10*
> *¹⁰ For with the heart one believes and is justified, and with the mouth one confesses and is saved.*
>
>
> *2 Corinthians 5:7*
> *⁷ for we walk by faith, not by sight.*

I don't need to provide any background on my cancer story here; I didn't provide much when I spoke, either, but focused instead on the difficulty in talking about it. My disease is not obvious from outside appearance, assuming I'm fully dressed, so cancer is something I must voluntarily expose when meeting new people, and I still worry, to some degree, about how this affects the way I'm regarded. Is cancer a pitiable weakness? Perhaps.

There are, of course, the physical and mental components: the broken body, the pain and discomfort, the difficulty of living a "regular life" with family and work, and the hindrances to serving others while bearing the guilt of being a burden, instead. But in many respects, this *is* regular life. I provide an account of my personal difficulties with cancer, but they're in no way limited to a life with cancer. Everyone experiences weaknesses of some sort; afflictions are a large part of what makes our lives unique.

But it is another form of weakness that consumes and drives me, the subject of so many blog posts, the mysterious but inescapable spirituality. It is this part of me that I feel we all share but is oddly the most difficult to talk about, as if the thing we have in common is what we must keep most private. In our youth, when our bodies and minds are capable and strong, there also, to varying degrees, a spiritual wonder exists, vibrant and imaginative, open to ideas of God. We grow up and out of much from our youth, but would we deny that we are made of mind, body, and soul? And if our bodies and minds are impacted by our experiences as we age, would we expect different of our souls? The soul can thrive, but it can also be scarred. In this I often dwell, revealing my weakness, my doubt and uncertainty, writing of the battle between my heart and head with belief in a Creator, in God, in Jesus. It is a blessing, indeed, that we are called to believe with our hearts (Romans 10:10) and live by faith (2 Cor 5:7), because we need not be held back from fruitfulness as we puzzle at life's great mysteries.

It is in the gift of faith that I've long sought to find purpose. I suspect I had once equated purpose with giftedness and giftedness with some personal strength, but through this battle, I have had to reconsider this. God being God and perhaps seeking to protect me from pride and self-glorification while providing the privilege to participate in His work, it makes sense that usefulness to God comes through our weakness, as demonstrated through Christ's death on a cross. Difficult as it has been to reveal in blog posts the many things I would ordinarily keep private, I have benefited not only from prayer and encouragement but also from words of gratitude from friends and family who relate to what I describe. This has been a great, unexpected blessing.

One of the difficulties in writing posts/essays/vignettes that often combine one's health problems, personal faith, Scripture verses, and a movie, book or other cultural reference is that it leaves much room for interpretation. I often wonder, what do readers of my posts think is the source of my periodic, deep anguish? In the previous post, "The 100th Sheep," what really made me cry at the post's end?

It is straightforward (and accurate) to point to the physical struggles, but these are ultimately the means by which my doubt in God's love is eroded as I experience His heart-breaking mercy. Frequently exhausted both body and soul, convicted as one who expects his Creator to prove himself in signs, I'm brought to tears in moments where I truly believe that he has. And it is here that I get the urge to write; yes, there is grief, but there is also a feeling of reassurance that there really is a good God weaving lives together for a much larger purpose. In reality, we can't really share each other's pain and sorrow, but we can certainly encourage each other with how God might be at work in our lives.

Please understand; I would not write blog posts to grumble or seek sympathy about what I'm going through with cancer. We all have our difficult circumstances. I only write about my difficulties when, in my weakness, I'm reminded of the strength that is given me in Christ to persevere. And those aren't mere words, at least to me, but an internal steeling that seems to appear out of nothing, a genesis of hope, strength and purpose that can only be explained by faith. You know, "Faith. F.A.I.T.H." This sort of thing hits you, and it brings you to your knees, to cry out of both pain and thankfulness. It may sound far-fetched to some, but the tears were real and that's how I explain it.

The bottom-line is that I would never have publicly delved so deeply into my personal weaknesses if I weren't proclaiming a greater strength in Christ, because, when the two are separated, I either feel ashamed of my weakness or like a religious nut, though, regardless, there is a bit of both of those feelings whenever I hit "Publish" on a post. So, while I humbly and gratefully invite friends and family to inquire about my health, I would rather talk about it in the context of faith, because then, in some way, the discussion isn't just about me, for the condition of our souls is a weakness that I believe we all share. And, if I'm right, this common weakness is where we find our greatest strength, somehow all things working together for our good, having been called according to God's purposes (Romans 8:28).

The good news is that this strength is not about our physical and mental attributes; rather, it is about our submission to God's will through our vulnerability. This sounds frightening and isn't easy to accept, but I suspect the call to be "conformed to the suffering servant" (Romans 8:29) is more than a spiritual endeavor. I'm imagining emotional and physical scars to be the marks of perseverance, and they have eternal permanence. *Eternal.*

Earlier, I told the story of Perceval because the restoration of the manly strength of his body is not something I relate to or even imagine. Ever. In this life, suffice to say that my wife has the privilege of sharing "one flesh" with a body of unique character, the battle having left its marks. And, like a knight I suppose, for my kids' sake as much as mine, I wear armor when-ever I'm around water, except mine is in the form of a rash guard. These scars of mine, I'll have them for the rest of this life, and if this life goes on after death and I'm ever brought back again into this body, I'll bear the scars then, too. Perceval's bodily restoration is not Gospel. The story of Christ's death and resurrection tells of a different type of restoration, one that gives me and all with faith in him a great hope that our lives here are not to be suffered as trial runs as we await new lives in the hereafter; they are the transformative part of our one eternal life.

Most everyone knows the story of Christ's crucifixion. Many know that the Bible tells of His resurrection. I don't know how many know that he bore the wounds from the nail piercings and a spear stab to his side after he rose from the dead. His body was not restored. What's even more interesting is that Jesus wasn't recognizable to his disciples until he showed them his wounds. Were they expecting a restoration that erased the proof of his suffering? Thomas, of doubting fame, had the audacity to demand to authenticate the risen Jesus by touching Christ's side. I can only speculate that his words smacked of sarcasm and that he must have been shamed to have Christ actually guide his hand to his ghastly sore. But Jesus was compassionate to Thomas and the others. And they recognized him by his wounds.

So, the Gospel teaches us that Jesus was known by his wounds, even beyond the grave. Jesus's wounds are a sign of his weaknesses and are permanent reminders of what he endured to love others. We should expect nothing less if we are to be conformed to him. We too are to be known by our wounds, by our worldly weaknesses. We are known to God by our suffering in Christ and thus to each other through the sharing of our struggles. Weakness, paradoxically, is the means by which we know God is for us because he strengthens us to love and serve others in the midst of it. In Christ, weakness is not to be hidden in shame or commiserated between the defeated but is the means through which we recognize and know one another and live by faith in promise of our future glory.

How far should this go? Do we want or need to know every detail about each other's lives? I don't think so, but we must be careful that we don't set each other up to only be of use in their strength. Consider the boss. Do you want to know about his or her colon function? Consider our pastors. Do you want to know about their marital problems? We may not need to know those sorts of details, but it certainly helps to understand them to know their spiritual side, scars and all; that's how I see it. Perhaps I'm in a unique situation where my work and social status is reasonably unaffected by what I divulge about myself, and I've invited others to share in my cancer story through these blog posts. That's my private, physical weakness. But I've also said plenty about my greatest weakness, that of needing a savior and yet always seeking to touch Jesus's side, so to speak, in looking for signs of his work to bolster my belief, rather than being thankful for the blessing of the faith bestowed. I admit I feel like most people can relate to this at some level. After all, if what the Bible says is true, then we all share that same weakness of the soul, to need a savior. And I think we need to talk about it. We need to know each other. We must be diligent about making our conversations less about us and our struggles in this world, solely, and more about thankfulness for fellowship between believers as we persevere together toward the world to come. Amen.

This may just be my final post, or at least my last post so focused on weakness. I feel I've said enough. I want to focus on the joys of this life, the benefits of faith. So, give me a call. Send me a text or an email. Let's get together. But let's not pretend we know each other as well as we ought. That might give me new material...

CT scan on Monday, Nov 20. Friends and family, we cherish your prayers. And we love you.

Many humble blessings.

*Romans 8:26-30*

*[26] Likewise the Spirit helps us in our weakness. For we do not know what to pray for as we ought, but*

*the Spirit himself intercedes for us with groanings too deep for words. <sup>27</sup> And he who searches hearts knows what is the mind of the Spirit, because the Spirit intercedes for the saints according to the will of God. <sup>28</sup> And we know that for those who love God all things work together for good, for those who are called according to his purpose. <sup>29</sup> For those whom he foreknew he also predestined to be conformed to the image of his Son, in order that he might be the firstborn among many brothers. <sup>30</sup> And those whom he predestined he also called, and those whom he called he also justified, and those whom he justified he also glorified.*

*Romans 10: 8-10*

*<sup>8</sup> But what does it say? "The word is near you, in your mouth and in your heart" (that is, the word of faith that we proclaim); <sup>9</sup> because, if you confess with your mouth that Jesus is Lord and believe in your heart that God raised him from the dead, you will be saved. <sup>10</sup> For with the heart one believes and is justified, and with the mouth one confesses and is saved.*

*2 Corinthians 5:6-7*

*<sup>6</sup> So we are always of good courage. We know that*

*while we are at home in the body we are away from the Lord, [7] for we walk by faith, not by sight.*

# Epilogue

Only cure or death would have been obvious stopping points, but, book-ended by two "Living Church" segments, it seemed the right time to publish this story so far, as told through the posts on my blog site (twostories.blog). But, because the end-point is somewhat arbitrary, I felt it necessary to provide some final thoughts. I feel like I've said enough about my faith, though. Having read through these posts as I assembled this book, I even wondered if it is too much. Preachy, didactic, repetitive, and ultimately boring. Only time will tell. But how to finish?

One night recently, as I lay in bed, I pondered the idea of coincidence, a theme that is frequent in my posts but which, I'm sure you know by now, I don't consider random occurrences. For a while now, I have documented remarkable coincidences in an unpublished "Blog of Coincidence." Most of the entries are recent, but I have incidents that date back to 2009. There are a few in particular that, to me, are mind-bogglingly unlikely by chance, but who knows? I considered whether I should have included any of them in this book, but I had decided against it. Setting aside these thoughts, I picked up my copy of Frederick Buechner's *Secrets in the Dark*, the collection of sermons from which I read "The Two

Stories." The book stays on my beside for occasional encouragement. This night, I thumbed through to find one that struck me, and I stopped on "Faith and Fiction," finding the title provocative but not remembering the subject. You won't be surprised to learn that the first three paragraphs describe incidents that fall into the category of either coincidence or some mysterious power at work in the world. I won't get into those he mentions, they're his after all, but about them he says:

> *"All that's extraordinary about these three minor events is the fuss I've made about them. Things like that happen every day to everybody. They are a dime a dozen. They mean absolutely nothing. Or things like that are momentary glimpses into a Mystery of such depth, power, and beauty that if we were to see it head-on, we would be annihilated."*

Upon reading his sermon, I was, of course, struck by the coincidence of reading a sermon on coincidences as I was considering including any of my stories about coincidence. But, alas, I wasn't swayed as to whether to mention any of them. That is, not until after breakfast the next morning. I was supposed to meet a friend at 7:45, and he had a tight schedule. Unfortunately, I ran late, so we were left with a mere twenty minutes to eat and chat (he ordered for me while I was in transit). Once I sat, set down my keys, poured myself a cup of coffee, and gave him my attention, essentially the first words out of his mouth were, "So, I know you don't be-

**332**

lieve in coincidences." He proceeded to tell me one of his coincidental stories.

I cry uncle. I'll end with three stories of coincidences. I'm sure you have many yourself. Good luck, bad luck or humdrum happenstance, even the most rational of storytellers sometimes sense a non-fictional force at work in this world.

The first story is one of many involving the number 26 (recall the post "Numbers"). Recently, my mother accompanied me to Nashville for my regular treatment. We enjoyed ourselves Sunday evening, but Monday was a long day. There were problems at the clinic which prolonged my visit, and our 5-hour trip took over 7. We didn't arrive at my mother's house until after 10 pm, and I was very tired from the day and the infusion of chemicals. My mother *really* wanted me to spend the night (moms, you know), but I insisted on going home (sons, you know). When I got in my car, I noticed that my phone battery was 26% (one-time occurrence, random, right?). I plugged in my phone and left for home. At the bottom of her long, winding driveway, I noticed that my car hadn't recognized my phone yet, so I stopped to check on it. As soon as I went to fiddle with the cable, my car info-screen refreshed, showing my phone, and, naturally, it was 10:26. I departed. Unfortunately, it wasn't an easy drive, as I met a road-block on the major highway and was forced to U-turn and take a detour. I'll add that I almost hit an armadillo and a pack of deer. You know where this is going. I walked in the door of my house right at 11:26, and I promise I didn't engineer this, though I saw it coming.

Another. In early January 2017, I received a text message from an unknown number saying that we needed to grab Waffle House sometime (he was referencing the "Mustard" post). I laughed and asked who it was. It was my cousin, who I then discovered lives near me but who I probably hadn't seen in 20+ years, though he and his father had been following my blog posts. We continued text-conversing, and, among other things, he informed me that he was a driver for FedEx. The following day, I found myself needing to make some phone calls, and, not wanting to disturb my office-mate, I walked down the hall to sit in one of the open, interaction zones (not an area I use often, by the way). When I finished my calls, I set my phone down on the armrest to think a moment. I then reached for my phone, the kind that illuminates the time, date and any notifications when it detects motion. OK, it was 10:26, but that isn't the shocker. At that exact moment, the doors to the nearby elevator opened, revealing first a hand truck stacked with FedEx boxes and then my cousin. 20+ years, some blog posts, a few text messages, the number 26, and out comes your cousin. I found out later that that was the first and only time he ever delivered packages to my building.

Finally, during a recent checkup, my oncologist excitedly informed my wife and me that the sponsoring drug company had advanced the protocol from the phase IB experimental trial on which I'm participating to a phase II study, thereby opening the treatment option to a larger group of people. The great news is that there will be more patients with colorectal cancer receiving this treatment and hopefully seeing their lives extended as I have. And, from a medical standpoint, even more exciting is that the new study will evaluate this treatment for patients whose disease has progressed after the first round of standard therapy (i.e. the cancer returned after initial treatment with standard chemotherapy). If successful, this would mean saving many more lives (many die from recurrent cancer after first- or second-line treatment). But this means I would not be a candidate for this treatment if I needed it today, because my disease progressed after two treatment protocols. As it turns out, the time window was narrow and the participants few for the current phase IB study. If I hadn't needed a third-line treatment in the fall of 2016, I'd either be on a completely different study (an alternative good result) or perhaps a victim of our worst fears. Who knows? But the timing of my visit to the oncologist in Nashville and her placing me on the hot, new trial was extremely fortunate. Now, every two weeks, a nurse hangs a couple of bags of clear chemicals on a chrome, cross-like contraption, standing passively on castors by my chair. Before starting the infusion pump, she asks a simple question to ensure that the correct person sits there. I answer, "Daniel Weatherly, five twenty-six seventy."

These stories I've told, they're deeply personal, but are they merely so? Or is there something more? Do we dare claim to glimpse the Creator at work in His Creation? Are there always Two Stories?

In "Faith and Fiction," Frederick Buechner, referring to the question of coincidence versus the supernatural, continued with this:

> *"If I had to bet my life on one possibility or the other, which one would I bet it on? If you had to bet your life, which one would you bet it on? On Yes, there is God in the highest, or, if such language is no longer viable, there is Mystery and Meaning in the deepest? On No, there is whatever happens to happen, and it means whatever you choose it to mean, and that is all there is?"*

Oh how thankful I am for God's mercy. My life would seem to have made the answer apparent, but, as you've read from my posts, I still struggle with the choice. Perhaps one day I'll be settled. Perhaps not. But as a nurse said to me in the clinic in another of my moments of doubt, "God's not through with you yet." He's not through with any of us, no matter the circumstances. I'd bet my life on it.

CPSIA information can be obtained
at www.ICGtesting.com
Printed in the USA
LVHW081914171119
637611LV00016B/459/P